Forage

Wild Plants to Gather, Cook and Eat

First published in Great Britain in 2021 by Laurence King
an imprint of The Orion Publishing Group Ltd
Carmelite House, 50 Victoria Embankment
London EC4Y 0DZ

An Hachette UK Company

10 9 8 7 6 5

A catalogue record for this book is available from the British Library.

ISBN: 978-1-78627-735-0

Commissioning editor: Zara Larcombe
Interior design: The Urban Ant
Cover design: Alex Wright
Author photograph on page 224: © Suzy Bennett

Disclaimer: Foraging wild ingredients requires expert knowledge and
identification. The publisher and author are not responsible for any
adverse effects or consequences resulting from the use, or misuse, of the
information contained in this book. The illustrations and text in this book
should not be used alone for identification purposes. So far as the author
is aware, the information given is correct and up-to-date as of June 2020.
Practice, laws and regulations all change, and the reader should obtain up-
to-date professional advice on any such issues.

Origination by Fine Arts Repro House
Printed in China by C&C Offset Printing Co. Ltd

www.laurenceking.com
www.orionbooks.co.uk

Forage

Wild Plants to Gather, Cook and Eat

Liz Knight

Illustrations by Rachel Pedder-Smith

Laurence King

CONTENTS

INTRODUCTION

Over 200,000 of the nearly 400,000 species of plants on earth are edible, from trees with leaves that make almond-tasting liqueurs, shrubs that are adorned with flowers full of the scent of coconut, to weeds that have roots that taste of cloves. This book is a mere glimpse into the incredibly delicious world of wild food, delving into 50 of the plants that make up a tiny part of the wild food that grows across the world. All of the plants featured in the book have been chosen not only because they are easy to identify, and abundant, but also because they are delicious and easy to use. No matter where in the temperate regions of the world you may be and regardless of whether you call the city or the countryside your home, many of the plants featured in this book are probably growing nearby. Divided into plant types – trees, shrubs and climbers, perennials, biennials and annuals – each plant is accompanied by detailed illustrations, and notes about when different parts are in season, what they taste like and a selection of recipes – some newly developed, others steeped in history, many laced with inspiration from foragers in far-away lands.

Why go foraging?

Forage is designed to ignite an excitement for foraging – not just because it is good for you (which it is) or because it is a sustainable way to eat (which it is) or because it is free (which it is) but mostly because the plants taste magical. Unique little mouthfuls which have the power to transform food from ordinary to joyful. And once you have mastered your first 50 plants, there is a lifetime ahead to discover the rest.

Foraging considerations

Before you reach for your foraging basket, there are a few things to consider as you head out.

Identification

It is an exhilarating experience to discover that there are so many wild foods within arm's reach, and the temptation to run out and eat everything can be strong, but before you begin your foray into becoming a gatherer of food, take time to properly identify plants – some plants are so toxic that a leaf will cause serious damage to vital organs or worse. Foraging is a lifetime of discovering new plants that you can eat, so only gather from the plants you 100 per cent know, and slowly broaden your knowledge. Some plants, especially perennials, shrubs and trees, change in their appearance through the year; getting to know plants from the early buds and shoots of spring to the dried seedheads of autumn will build your confidence in your ability to identify plants accurately – before long your eyes will become adept at seeing different species of plants that grow in what once might have seemed to be a blanket of green.

You'll notice on the pages that follow some of the plants' scientific names are followed by 'spp.', this indicates that there are more than one edible species of that plant (other than the one illustrated), but this does not necessarily mean that all the other species of the plant are safe to eat.

Allergy awareness
Remember each body is unique, and reacts to foods in different ways. Once you have identified a plant that is edible, introduce small amounts into your diet at first to make sure that you do not have a negative reaction to it. Don't let this scare you off though; very few of us can tolerate all conventional foods, and wild ingredients are no different. And if you have a known allergy to a specific food such as mustard or celery, it is advised that you avoid their wild relatives. (Mustard family plants in this book are hairy bittercress, garlic mustard and horseradish. Hogweed and ground elder are related to celery). Approach eating wild plants with care if you are on specific medications in case the plants can react with your medication or affect your condition. Again, this is true of many conventional foods and medications; seek advice from your doctor or a qualified medical herbalist; if you are unsure if a plant may affect you, don't eat it. Finally, if you are pregnant or breastfeeding, exercise real caution with wild food. Use your pregnancy and hours of walking your baby to sleep to learn about the food you will be able to enjoy once your baby is older.

Foraging responsibly and legally
Across the world there are different rules and regulations about the harvesting of wild plants. In England and Wales, for example, you can gather wild plants, apart from protected species, for personal use, from public land (unless the area falls within a protected area such as a Site of Special Scientific Interest – SSSI). It is only lawful in England and Wales to uproot a plant if you have the land owner's permission, an important fact to keep in mind for plants that have edible roots. Read up on your local regulations, and follow your area's rules.

Forage what you need
Alongside local rules, bear in mind that plants are here not only for us, but to support and feed a wide range of other animals. A responsible forager gathers only as much as they need, and only from an area where a plant is not scarce. A good rule to follow is to gather in a way that when you look back at where you have been picking, it looks no different to before you went there. As tempting as it is to load up with a huge hoard of a crop, think about what you are going to do with your haul when you get home. If you find that you have bags of harvested leaves and fruits going mouldy before you use them, you probably have gathered too much. One of the joys of wild food is that what you can collect changes week by week; small amounts of lots of flavours is far more exciting in your cupboards than a huge amount of one flavour.

You may have a beautiful foraging basket to take with you on your outings, but more useful than one large receptacle is a number of little bags so that your inevitable selection of gatherings are not all mixed up with each other; cloth bags are ideal, as they are breathable and are easier to stuff into your pocket when you're on an impromptu foraging trip. A sturdy pair of scissors is useful to snip at your finds, as are a pair of gardening gloves for handling those more prickly customers. A shepherd's crook is handy for gently bending down branches laden with blooms, fruit and nuts.

Getting the most out of your finds

Not much can beat eating food that is freshly harvested; the flavours of freshly gathered herbs in a salad is a treat anyone who has grown their own food will know. But there is also delight to be had in gathering your own wild pantry, preserving the best of the flavours of the changing seasons for the months ahead. You can preserve plants in any manner of ways; each technique will produce a different flavour and texture, and some plants are more suited to one form rather than another; in the 'Cook and Eat' sections there are suggestions suited to the specific plant, but they are by no means exhaustive; wild food provides the perfect opportunity to experiment.

Drying

Drying foods is a fantastic way to preserve them for later in the year. You do not need a dehydrator: you can dry tender herbs and flowers on a warm radiator and thicker items, or fruits, in a low oven, but the shelves and low temperature of a dehydrator make it incredibly useful in a wild kitchen. You do not need an expensive or large dehydrator, but if you anticipate using it a lot, it is worth buying the best you can afford. Dry delicate herbs and flowers on the lowest possible setting until the dry plants crumble (this can take a few hours). Some plants reabsorb moisture very quickly, so once your flowers or herbs are dry place them in an airtight jar and keep them in a dry, cupboard away from direct light. They can be stored like this for up to a year; even if you have not used up all of your herbs from the previous year, discard older herbs once the new year's plant is ready to harvest. Dried herbs are concentrated versions of the fresh plants: 10g of dried, powdered nettle, for example, equates to roughly 120g of fresh nettle.

Fermentation

This age-old tradition both preserves food and maximizes its nutritional content; fermentation is the act of allowing certain bacteria and acids to grow, creating an environment that inhibits dangerous bacteria from developing. It can be done using salt, yeasts or, in dairy products, specific bacterial cultures. A by-product of fermentation using salts – used to make pickles, kimchi and sauerkraut – is vitamin C; pickled cabbage, for example, has ten times more vitamin C than fresh cabbage, alongside health-giving probiotics. Besides pickles, fermentation is used in making everything from wines and beers to yoghurts and naturally carbonated drinks such as flower champagnes, which are fermented for a few days and produce only the slightest hint of alcohol.

Whatever you decide to ferment though, all ferments require scrupulously clean equipment and storage vessels. To ensure your tools are squeaky clean, wash your equipment thoroughly in hot, soapy water (or on the hottest dishwasher setting) and dry with a clean tea-towel (freshly laundered in a boil wash). Dry glass or metal equipment in a low oven. To be doubly sure your equipment is thoroughly clean, submerge the washed items in a bowl of water with sterilizing solution added (use the kind sold for babies' bottles), following the manufacturer's instructions and timings.

Preserving

Preserving your finds, especially fruits in jellies or jams, is a beautiful way to have wild flavours available all year round. Discard any fruit that is blemished or starting to rot; if the fruit is softening significantly, preserve it by dehydration rather than in a jelly or jam, as very ripe fruits are more likely to spoil. It can be tempting to make huge batches of preserves, but avoid making too much of one type of jam, unless you want to give lots away to friends and family. It is far more enjoyable to have shelves lined with lots of little batches of different flavours that reflect your foraging year. When you make jams or syrups, look at other plants that are in season at the same time as your main ingredient; sweet things are ideal vehicles for pairing flavours; cherry and almond scented meadowsweet jam is so delicious it might've come from another realm, and late summer honeysuckle flowers infused into damson jam add a floral squeal of delight to the deeply fruity damsons.

A sugar thermometer is really useful for testing the temperature of jellies and jams, and to make caramels, candies and marshmallow sweets. If you haven't got one, you can use the tried and tested 'wrinkle test' for jellies and jams to check the set – drop a small amount of your preserve on a cold plate and push your finger through it; a wrinkled appearance means your preserve will set.

Once you have made your preserves, pour them whilst very hot into warmed, sterile jars or bottles, leaving a head space of ½cm between the preserve and the lid, making sure that there are no air bubbles in the jar and that there are no drops of your preserve on the rim of the jar, or this will affect the seal and could let bacteria into the preserve. Seal your jars with sterilized, dry lids. You can store your preserves in a fridge or even freezer (leave a larger gap between the preserve and the lid if you are freezing).

Pasteurizing

If you would like to be able to store your preserves for longer without filling up the freezer, a final step in ensuring a long shelf life is pasteurization. This can be done by placing your filled and lidded jars into a pan of boiling water which has a rack or a folded tea towel at the bottom for the jars to stand on. Make sure the pan has enough water in it to cover the jars by a couple of centimetres. Carefully place the jars into the pan, making sure they don't tilt on their way in, turn up the heat to bring the water to boil for at least 10 minutes before carefully removing the jars; again do not let them tilt and place them on an even surface to rest until cool.

Pasteurizing like this is suitable for high acid, low pH preserves such as pickles, many jams and syrups or cordials. Low acid foods need specialized canning equipment to preserve them safely. If you want to preserve with pasteurization, you will find a pH monitor becomes an indispensable piece of kit. You can pick these up quite cheaply, and they are incredibly useful to ensure food safety of anything that you are preserving other than by dehydration. To preserve food safely you need to achieve a pH of lower than 4.6, ideally lower still if you are preserving in oil. This creates an environment that inhibits growth of harmful pathogens.

What awaits you

Other than clean equipment, and a few preserving tricks, what you really need for a successful foraging outing is a little bit of time. Understand that once you have discovered your inner forager, there won't be any going back. If you can accept the fact that for ever more you'll get hungry at the sight of the first weeds of spring, that you'll rubberneck trees laced in blossom and dripping in fruit, that you'll find it hard to leave the house without a spare bag, just in case you happen to come across something at the peak of its season, then you are equipped to begin. Prepare for the untidy verges, overgrown derelict areas, and weedy gardens to suddenly change in your mind's eye to the most beautiful, abundant of places and for the world to seem that bit more delicious.

TREES

Trees are not only the lungs of the earth, they
are also the pantry. Providing everything from
mineral-rich sap, to tender salad leaves, blossoms
and flowers that can be used for flavouring and
medicine, through to nuts that can be used
as oils, gluten-free flour and liqueurs.
Whilst trees are here, we can breathe easy.

BIRCH

Betula spp.

Birch are pioneering species; one of the first trees that grew after the
last Ice Age, they repopulated the thawing tundra. With a unique ability
to fix nitrogen in nodules found on their roots, they were able to
survive and thrive on the poorest of soils. Birch trees swiftly established
colonies of fast-growing trees in the barren, depleted ground. Their
slender forms cast a dappled shade, nourishing the earth with fallen
leaves, aerating the soil with their wide-spreading roots, forming
swathes of light-filled woodland and providing a protective arm around
the area to encourage slower-growing species to eventually grow into
the long-lived ancient woodlands we know today.

Birch trees have an equally nourishing relationship with people;
across the Northern Hemisphere birch has been used for millennia
to provide shelter, tools, medicine and food. For hundreds of years,
people have drunk birch sap in the spring – a season when fresh food
was traditionally at its most scarce – providing a sweet drink full of
nourishing properties, a spring tonic from the tree.

Whilst the sap rises through the tree, herbalists gather swelling leaf
buds which are used as herbal antibiotics; once open, the young leaves
are used as a cleansing green tea, and catkins and twigs are turned
into bitter tonics. When they reach old age, northern-living trees can
play host to immune-boosting fungi chaga (*Inonotus obliquus*), and
dying trunks provide a home for horseshoe-shaped birch polypore
(*Piptoporus betulinus*), used to make primitive wound dressings and
medicine. Birch may live fast and die young, but even in its demise it
keeps sharing its treasures.

Slender pendulous twigs that are traditionally used in making brooms. The tender tips can be infused into bitters; the buds are used in herbal medicines.

Small, triangular, toothed leaves ending in a pointed tip, opening in early spring and turning yellow in the autumn. The young opened leaves can be gathered and used as a green tea.

Leaf buds form during the winter months, swelling as the sap starts rising. Once the leaves start opening, the flow of sap slows down and the season to gather the sweet liquid is over for the year.

Betula pendula

BIRCH

Birch sap was historically used fresh and fermented, both as a watery sweet drink and turned into ale, wine and vinegar. It was often paired with other flavours, including gooseberry, dill and cherry.

Reducing birch sap produces a versatile, deeply flavoured syrup, with fruity molasses and liquorice notes. It is delicious used as a flavouring in small amounts. Young leaves make a delicious green tea, while older leaves and catkins are good for woody, deeply flavoured bitters.

HOW TO TAP FOR BIRCH SAP

- Strong string/rope
- Demijohns or large bottles with handles
- Branch loppers

For a few weeks each spring, just before the leaves open, you can harvest the fast-flowing birch sap that is being pulled up into the tips of the birch tree. As ground water pulls through the xylem layer of the tree, so it absorbs sugars stored in this layer, just under the inner bark, becoming sweeter as it reaches the leaf buds. Early records reveal that people chopped down whole trees to gather the sap; if you have seen a cut tree in spring you'll see how much sap pours from it. Many people drill holes a couple of inches into the tree, harvesting the sap from the trunk, but for the least intrusive, sweetest harvest, reach for the ends of the slim limbs.

1. At the end of winter, every few days break off the end of a tip of a birch twig – if a bead of water appears at the break, the sap is rising.

2. Find a low-hanging branch and lop off the end of it, so that it can fit into the end of the bottle. Push the branch at least 10cm in, making sure the bottle opening is facing upwards. Tie rope through the handles of the bottle and attach securely to the branch. The sweet sap will drip into the bottle; with a good flow it can fill up within 48 hours. Leave the sap for no more than 48 hours, or it will start to ferment (see syrup recipe opposite if this happens).

3. Pour the sap into freezer-proof bottles and freeze until needed.

BIRCH SAP SYRUP
(FOR PEOPLE WITH EITHER GALLONS
OR A FEW LITRES OF SAP)

Makes 300ml

- 250g unrefined sugar
- 2 litres birch sap

Birch sap syrup is made by reducing the sap from the tree by 80 times its original volume. You can significantly reduce the simmering required by freezing birch sap and only using the first quarter of the sap that thaws – this will include the sugars that you need to make syrup.

If you have a lot of sap, in a wide pan, slowly simmer it until it reduces to a caramel-brown liquid, tasting similar to pomegranate molasses. Take extreme care not to boil away all the sap, resulting in burnt pans and tears.

If you have only a smaller quantity of sap, you can still use the flavour of birch in a syrup, just follow the recipe below, with the helping hand of unrefined sugar.

1. Add a teaspoon of the sugar to a 2-litre bottle of birch sap, then leave in a warm, light place until it starts fermenting – it will turn cloudy and start to smell sour and yeasty (often within a day or so).

2. Pour the sour liquid into a large, wide pan and warm over a medium heat. Pour in the rest of the sugar and stir to dissolve. Slowly reduce the sap to a thick golden colour and a syrup consistency. The resulting syrup is lighter in taste and colour than maple syrup, and is delicious on pancakes.

BIRCH BITTERS – BJORK
Makes 500ml

- Enough birch twigs, leaves and catkins to loosely fill a wide-necked lidded 1-litre jar
- 750ml vodka

When the sap stops flowing, it is time to gather newly emerged leaves, catkins and twigs to make Bjork, a traditional Icelandic bitter drink that is cleaner and more versatile than angostura bitters. Bjork can be sweetened with birch syrup, or used as a bitter by itself. Birch bitters also work beautifully with the addition of caraway, cardamom or liquorice.

1. Place the birch twigs and any other ingredients into a jar, pour over the vodka, making sure that no plant matter sticks above the alcohol.

2. Store in a dark cupboard – after a few days the vodka will be astringent, grassy tasting and bitter. Leave for up to 3 months to macerate, during which time the tannic woodiness of the bark will leach out, creating a smooth whisky-like bitter that is good enough to drink by itself.

WILD CHERRY

Prunus spp.

Look skywards in a broadleaf woodland in early spring and you will
find blossom-covered cherry trees. In open settings cherry trees
spread widely with low-hanging branches, but in the woods they
turn into slim, tall giants stretching up to access light. The abundance
of wild cherry trees is only really displayed during cherry blossom
season, when other, slower-to-wake species are often still bare. Once
you find the blossom-frosted trees, put a reminder in your diary to
make regular trips back in the summer. If you can find low-hanging
branches you will be able to gather cherries. Although most of
the cherries you will find in the wild woods are from the original
uncultivated forms, you may sometimes find large, tooth-achingly
sweet fruits. The presence of both wild and cultivated cherries in woods
is down to the same reason that trees laden with fruit one day are bare
the next – birds. Birds gorge on the fruit of wild and orchard-grown
hybrids alike, often swallowing seeds whole before flying to woodland
roosts, where they drop the seed, having passed it first through their
stone-filled grinding gullets and acidic stomachs, stripping off the hard
outer-coating shell, allowing the seed to germinate.

The survival and spread of cherry trees is very much down to these
birds, who are lured by the fruits' bright colours. So important are
the birds to the spread of cherry trees that the fruit has evolved to
benefit from being plundered and eaten by them, requiring the brutal
treatment it gets as it passes through their bodies in order to germinate,
spreading the trees further across woodlands, seas and lands.

Although we cannot help the tree to spread by grinding stones in
our gizzards, the cherry tree provides us with huge benefits, because
not only are the fruit delicious, they are also packed full of vitamin
C, beta carotene, vast amounts of minerals, melatonin, blood-sugar-
lowering abscisic acid, fibre and antioxidants. Just remember during
your gathering spree to leave some for the birds.

Wild cherry trees can grow to over 30 metres tall; the tallest trees are often within woodlands. The bark of young cherry trees has horizontal blisters along the trunk, helping with identification of the tree in winter. Bark is used in medicinal teas.

Growing alternately along twigs, the young leaves emerge reddish green, glossy and tacky feeling, turning green and growing larger with toothed edges. Young leaves are used to wrap sticky rice dishes in Japan in the spring.

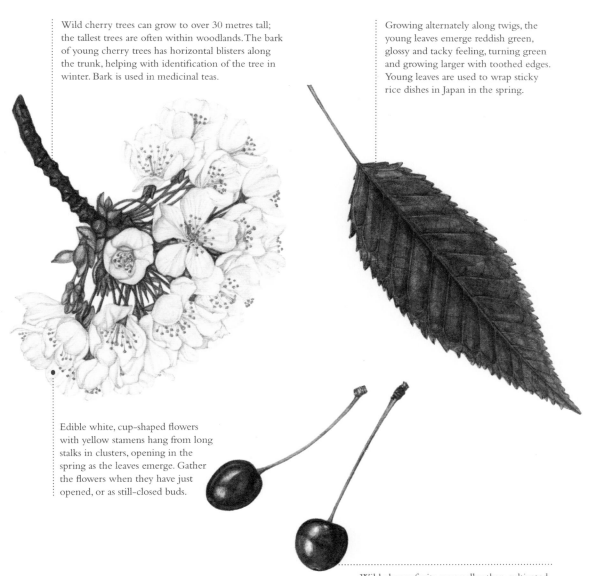

Edible white, cup-shaped flowers with yellow stamens hang from long stalks in clusters, opening in the spring as the leaves emerge. Gather the flowers when they have just opened, or as still-closed buds.

Caution: Only gather fresh flowers, leaves and bark, discarding any that have fallen from the tree and wilted. Although a small amount of cherry stones can be used as flavouring if carefully processed, avoid consuming stones directly.

Wild cherry fruits are smaller than cultivated cherries, turning from green to bright red or dark purple when ripe. Wild cherries produce a small, round stone which you will often find scattered at the base of the trees after birds have eaten the fruits. Look up and you may find you are standing under the tree that provides your following year's cherry harvest.

Prunus avium

WILD CHERRY

Cherry blossom is less familiar as an edible treat than the fruit, but it is equally delicious. Its exquisite flavour has hints of almond as well as a bitter cherry perfume and it is lovely when infused into panna cottas, cakes, syrups, and savoury salts. The cherries themselves make fantastic pickles, preserved in sweetened vinegar with a hint of warming spice.

CHERRY AND MEADOWSWEET CLAFOUTIS
Serves 4

- 450g cherries, pitted and halved
- 6 tbsp sugar, plus extra for sprinkling
- 3 tbsp kirsch (optional)
- 1 sprig of fresh or dried meadowsweet flowers
- 20g unsalted butter, plus extra for greasing
- 2 free-range organic eggs
- ½ tsp vanilla extract
- 1 heaped tbsp plain flour
- 50ml full-fat milk
- 75ml whipping cream, plus extra to serve
- Pinch of salt

Meadowsweet flowers and cherries are in season at the same time; the almond scent of meadowsweet pairs beautifully with cherries.

1. Mix the cherries, 3 tbsp of sugar, kirsch and meadowsweet sprig together in a bowl and leave to macerate for 2 hours.

2. Preheat the oven to 180°C, 350°F, gas mark 4. Grease a baking dish with butter and sprinkle over some sugar.

3. Heat the butter in a pan until it turns a pale golden brown, then remove from the heat.

4. Whisk the eggs, the remaining sugar and vanilla until light and creamy. Whisk in the flour and then slowly add the milk, cream and melted butter. Fold the cherries (and macerating liquid) into the batter and pour into the buttered dish. Bake for 30–35 minutes; the clafoutis is ready when a knife inserted into the centre of the mixture comes out clean.

5. Serve warm with whipped cream with cherry liqueur.

PICKLED JAPANESE CHERRY BLOSSOMS – SAKURA

Makes 100g

....

- 150g cherry blossom buds
- 50g preservative-free salt
- 500ml Ume (Japanese plum vinegar) or apple cider vinegar

....

Months before the cherry fruit ripen, the tree offers a harvest of flowers and leaves, known as Sakura in Japan.

1. Gather tender young leaves and tightly closed buds and soak overnight in water.

2. The next day drain the blossoms and leaves, shaking them to remove excess water. Sprinkle with salt, ensuring that all the leaves and flowers are coated. Place in a glass or stoneware container and press down the blossoms and leaves with a weight. Let sit for four days in a cupboard. The salt will draw out water from the blossoms, making a brine. Check each day to make sure that nothing is above the brine (remove any blossoms or leaves that are floating above the brine).

3. After the fourth day, drain the blossoms and leaves and discard the brine. Cover in Ume (Japanese plum vinegar) or cider vinegar, and leave for a further four days before draining. Spread out on a tray and leave to dry before tossing the pickled blossoms in a teaspoon of salt and storing in an air-tight container.

4. To remove the preserving salt, rinse the flowers before use. (If you are using the flowers in sweet dishes, soak the blossoms to remove any saltiness.)

SOUR CHERRY DRINK – SHARBAT E ALBALOO

Makes 500ml

....

- 400g pitted sour cherries
- 200g sugar
- 500ml water
- 2 tsp rose water (or petals from 2 fragrant roses)

....

The first cherries are thought to have originated from between the Black and Caspian Seas, where sour cherries in particular form a treasured part of the region's cuisine. Sharbats are sour, fruity and refreshing drinks, and the inspiration behind today's sherbet sweets.

1. Place the sour cherries, sugar, water and rose water or rose petals in a heavy-based pan, bring to the boil and then turn the heat to low and cook slowly until the juices thicken into a syrup. Pour the mixture into a large-enough jar that the cherries can fit in as well and chill, or pasteurize (see page 9) in bottles to keep for up to 6 months.

2. To serve the drink, strain enough syrup from your jar to be able to dilute 1 part syrup with 3 parts ice-cold water, or turn it into a sherbet ice by adding milk rather than water and freezing it as you would a sorbet. The leftover cherries are delicious stirred into ice cream or served with yoghurt.

HAWTHORN

Crataegus spp.

❧ DISTRIBUTION

Native to Europe, Asia,
North Africa, naturalized in
North and South America
and Australia.

❧ HABITAT

Hedgerows, fields, edges
of woodland.

**❧ GATHERING
SEASONS**

Early spring:
Young opened leaves.

Mid-spring:
Flower buds and
open flowers.

Late summer–late autumn:
Ripe fruits.

Once upon a time, the Celtic goddess Olwen walked an empty universe; wherever Olwen walked, flowers bloomed, leaving clouds of hawthorn blossom in her wake. Legend tells that the blossoms she lost to the skies stayed suspended there, turning into the Milky Way. A romantic myth, perhaps, but look at rural landscapes across the world during mid-spring and the trails of blossom transform green hedgerows into a reflection of the white swathes of faraway galaxies. They may produce starry-eyed gazes but the tracks of white are there for a far less dreamy, more practical reason; the thorny, gnarled tree behind the blossom provided an ideal livestock-proof hedging plant, which is why hawthorn is in nearly every hedgerow, even in lands where the tree was not native. As European farmers took livestock to America, New Zealand and Australia, they also transported European species of hawthorn saplings as stock-proof fencing. In their new environment, the trees spread across the landscape, often acting as an invasive species, crowding out native trees and gaining a far less ethereal reputation than it held in its homelands, where for thousands of years the tree had been associated with magic, miracles, myths and folklore.

Whether you regard it as invasive or magical, the benefits of eating from the tree might make you see hawthorn as just a bit miraculous. The leaves, blossom and berries are all edible and almost as supernatural as its folklore; extraordinarily rich in immune-boosting, circulation-supporting antioxidants, blood cell and heart-protecting flavonoids; food fit for universe-wandering goddesses.

With deeply toothed leaves, growing up to 6cm in length, hawthorns are some of the first hedging plants to form leaves in the spring. Initially vibrant green, turning darker as they age, hawthorn leaves can be eaten raw in the spring, and as they mature can be used for teas.

Sweetly scented, five-petalled white or occasionally pink flowers. Most hawthorn blossoms can be used in teas and as flavourings. Some older varieties, however, are pollinated by putrid-smell-loving flies, so use your senses to work out if the blossom is worth gathering.

Clusters of little, slightly oval, shiny red fruit. Like apples and pears, hawthorn berries have star-shaped remains of the flower on the base of the fruit. Inside the fruit the flesh is creamy coloured, starchy and grainy textured like an avocado, surrounding a large seed.

Caution: Hawthorn seeds are toxic and should not be consumed (it is safe to cook the berry with the seed, if you discard the seed before eating). Hawthorn is a proven heart medicine, so seek medical advice before consuming hawthorn if you have a cardiac illness, in case of reaction to medications.

Crataegus monogyna

HAWTHORN

Across Europe, Asia, the Middle East and America different species of hawthorn are eaten and drunk, often in jams, sauces or sweets – from chilli-spiked rielitos, candies served in Mexico on the Day of the Dead, to haw flakes, made in China. The fruits' sweet and sour tang is also delicious in savoury dishes.

HAWTHORN FLOWER SYRUP
Makes 250ml

- 250g sugar
- 1-litre jug half-filled with freshly gathered, newly opened hawthorn flowers
- Juice of ½ lemon

In northern Europe and America, hawthorn often explodes into blossom in May. So reliable is the blossom's timing, that hawthorn is known in Britain as the May tree. On May Day, women would head out in the morning to wash their faces in the dew which had collected overnight in the blossoms, hoping that the legend about the blossoms granting youthfulness and beauty was true. Folk tales often contain some elements of truth and the antioxidants in the flowers, leaves and berries all help remove free radicals that lead to ageing. If finding your everlasting youth at sunrise seems too early to wake up for, you can infuse the flowers into a syrup that captures the benefits and flavour of the blossom, and enjoy its delicious properties later in the day.

1. Heat 250ml of water and the sugar in a pan, bringing to the boil and stirring until the sugar has dissolved and the liquid is clear. Leave to cool for 10 minutes, and when slightly cooled pour over the hawthorn flowers, adding the lemon juice.

2. Press the flowers into the warm syrup; if the blossoms come to the surface, weigh them down with a small lid or water-filled food bag. Cover and leave to infuse overnight.

3. The next day, strain and pour into sterilized bottles. Store in the fridge or freeze in ice cube trays.

Hawthorn flower syrup is beautiful with Greek yoghurt, drizzled over almond cakes or fluffy pancakes, or used as a flavouring in homemade Turkish delight. You can make the most delicious cocktail to celebrate the coming of May by lightly muddling a handful of gorse and elderflower blossoms with ice in a cocktail shaker, then adding 20ml of the syrup, a squeeze of lemon, soda water and, if you like, a glug of gin. Shake and enjoy a drink that is as refreshing as early summer dew.

HAWTHORN BREAD AND CHEESE TOASTED GREMOLATA

Makes 8–10 servings

- 2 tsp olive oil
- 100g stale bread, blended into crumbs
- 2 tbsp finely grated Parmesan
- 2 tbsp finely chopped young hawthorn leaves
- 1 tsp lemon zest
- Salt and freshly ground black pepper

Hawthorn leaves were eaten across Britain by rural children, who nibbled them on their way to school. They were known as Bread and Cheese – quite why is a mystery, as hawthorn leaves don't taste like either bread or cheese, but they happen to taste delicious with both in a toasted gremolata. Crispy breadcrumbs with Parmesan can season and give crunch to pastas, sauces, vegetables and meats, and are well worth gathering hawthorn leaves for.

1. Heat the olive oil in a frying pan. As soon as the oil is hot, add the breadcrumbs, stirring all the time until they have turned golden and started to become crunchy. Remove from the heat and cool.

2. Once cool, add the cheese, hawthorn and lemon zest. Season and serve or store in an airtight jar in the fridge for up to a week.

HAWTHORN BERRY MARINADE

Makes about 300ml

- 250g hawthorn berries, washed
- 160ml honey or 160g light brown sugar
- 125ml soy sauce
- 2 tsp toasted sesame oil
- 1 tbsp rice wine vinegar
- 3 tbsp minced fresh root ginger
- 2 tbsp minced garlic
- 1 red chilli, finely chopped
- Salt

Hawthorn berries that grow in Asia are the size of small apples and are often eaten as dessert, simmered to extract their juice or candied like toffee apples. Hawthorn's sweet and sour flavours are delicious paired with Asian flavours of ginger and soy, and make an incredible sauce for dipping or marinating vegetables, tofu and meats.

1. Put the hawthorn berries in a pan and cover with water, then cook over a gentle heat until soft and pulpy (depending on the ripeness of the berries, this can take 10–30 minutes). Press the berries through a sieve, reserving the cooking water, and return the pulped flesh and water to the pan. Add the remaining ingredients and cook, stirring until the sugar has dissolved and the ingredients are blended together. Reduce to a thick paste, pour into sterilized jars and store in the fridge for up to a month.

SPRUCE

Picea spp.

You may know spruce as 2-metre Christmas trees, but leave them to grow into their prime and they become giants – up to 60 metres high – and in the right location they can live for thousands of years: the oldest living tree in the world is thought to be a spruce in the Swedish mountains, which started growing 9,000 years ago.

Surviving the long, bitter winters for such a length of time is no mean feat, but spruce trees are well adapted to long lives and cool climates. The conical shape of the tree might make it delightful to look at with fairy lights on, but its design is more practical, allowing snow to roll off the branches without breaking them. The long thin needles also assist in its survival, clinging onto the tree for years, they allow the tree to photosynthesize through the winter; the sugar produced in the winter leaves acts as an antifreeze and prevents the tree from dying in the cold.

The cleverly designed spruce not only sustains itself during the bleak winter months but is also a supply of citrus-flavoured vitamin C for people – a vitamin much lacking when the snow covers most other green crops. So concentrated is the vitamin C in spruce that simple cups of needle tea have been known to save the lives of scurvy suffering sailors, who arrived in bitterly cold snow-covered lands after gruelling voyages. After spruce tea brought them back from the brink of an early death, they probably would have felt like decorating the lifesaving trees whether it was Christmas or not.

Each spring, new tips grow at the end of twigs, covered with a papery brown casing that blows away as the tips grow larger. The young, vitamin-C-laden tips are tender when they first emerge and will stay soft enough to eat in salads for only a few days before they harden, when they are best used as an infusion or flavouring.

Spruce trees have four-sided, needle-like leaves that stay on the tree for up to ten years, growing individually around twigs, unlike other kinds of pine trees, which grow longer needles in clusters.

Caution: spruce trees are members of the pine family of coniferous trees, many of which are edible. However, another coniferous tree, the yew, is deadly poisonous. Prior to gathering from any conifer species, be able to identify a yew tree.

Picea abies

SPRUCE

All spruce, and other pine varieties, have slightly different citrus flavours; from grapefruit to lemon, they provide a fruity, acidic flavouring to sweet and savoury food. The newly open tips are tender enough to add sparingly to salads or wilt into buttery sauces, providing acidity to cut through the fat. Prolonged cooking destroys the flavour of spruce, so if the tips are going to be cooked, add them at the end of cooking as you would a fresh herb. Young spruce tips are delicious in ice creams, sorbets and cakes; slightly older, tougher tips are great ground into salts and sugars. As the needles age they can be used in vitamin-C-rich herbal teas and vinegars. The young cones can be preserved in syrups and vinegars or added to dishes raw.

RHUBARB AND SPRUCE COMPOTE
Makes 500g

- 500g rhubarb, chopped into 5cm chunks
- 75g sugar
- 20g young spruce tips, finely chopped, or a short sprig of older needles attached to the stem

Rhubarb and spruce capture the vibrant flavours of spring. This sharp compote is delicious dolloped on yoghurt and oats for breakfast, or topped with a crumble mixture, and is sharp enough to serve as a sauce alongside savoury dishes.

1. Preheat the oven to 180°C, 350°F, gas mark 4.

2. Place the rhubarb in a baking dish with a splash of water, spoon over the sugar and coat the chunks. Cut a piece of baking paper to fit over the rhubarb, then place in the oven for 30 minutes or until the rhubarb starts collapsing.

3. Cool until the rhubarb is warm and gently fold in the spruce tips. (Or push the whole stem into the rhubarb and leave to infuse for at least 2 hours before removing.) Spoon into sterilized jars and store in the fridge for up to a week.

SPRUCE PRESERVE

Makes 100ml syrup and 150g sugar paste

....

- 200g sugar
- 100g spruce needles and/or green cones
- 25ml water

....

Both spruce needles and cones have traditionally been made into thick, dark syrups. Packed into glass jars with an equal amount of sugar to spruce, they are left in the sun for a couple of months to transform into a pine-flavoured syrup, which is delicious in baking and cocktails. If you don't have time to 'sun bake' your spruce, use your oven to turn sugar and tree into a honeyed syrup in just a few hours.

1. Stir 100g of the sugar and the spruce into the water in a heatproof bowl. Press a disc of baking parchment over the ingredients and cover with a lid. Place the bowl in an oven set to 70°C, 150°F, gas mark ¼, for at least 3 hours, or until the sugar has turned into a thick syrup.

2. Strain the honey-flavoured syrup from the spruce and pour into a sterilized bottle. Store in a cool, dark place for up to a year.

3. The remaining spruce tips and cones will still contain a lot of citrus flavour. Sprinkle the spruce the remaining 100g of sugar and blend in a food processor to make a spruce sugar paste that can be used in baking.

SPRUCE AND WALNUT MINCEMEAT

Makes 650g

....

- 100g shelled wet or dried walnuts
- 250g peeled russet apples
- 250g raisins
- 300ml sloe gin
- 50g sugar
- A handful of spruce sprigs

....

Since the first trees were decorated in Germany in the sixteenth century, Christmas and spruce trees have been inextricably linked; the scent of pine fills houses at Christmas and if you source an untreated tree, snip off a few sprigs to make a mincemeat that tastes as Christmassy as your tree.

1. Chop the walnuts and russet apples into small pieces. Add to a bowl with the raisins, pour over the gin, stir in the sugar and taste to check for sweetness.

2. Press the sprigs fully into the mixture, cover and leave to infuse for 3–4 days, tasting every so often. The spruce flavour will start to permeate the gin, nuts and fruit. When the spruce flavour is distinct but not overpowering, remove the sprigs and place the fruit and nuts in sterilized jars to use at Christmas. There will be quite a lot of liquid left at the bottom of the bowl – pour it into a glass and leave out for Father (or Mother) Christmas to enjoy on Christmas Eve.

BEECH

Fagus spp.

◖ DISTRIBUTION

Europe, Asia, North America.

◖ HABITAT

Moist, well-drained soil in broadleaf woodlands. Beech grows especially well on chalky and limestone soils.

◖ GATHERING SEASONS

Spring:
Young, newly emerged leaves – gather until the leaves become opaque.

Autumn:
Nuts (known as masts), older leaves.

Living for up to 1,000 years and growing to heights of 40 metres, beech trees are woodland giants. Their branches reach as wide as they do high and the light that filters through the almost translucent, newly opened leaves creates emerald cathedrals. Indeed, the boughs of beech trees are said to have inspired the architecture of domed ceilings in places of worship.

Beech trees play a long and starring role in many deciduous woodlands, from mid-spring when the silken, lemon-flavoured young leaves line the delicate ends of branches like bunting, to when they age and become darker and denser. Beech woodlands provide the ideal home to the most shade-tolerant and often very rare plants, including the almost-extinct, chlorophyll-free ghost orchid. It's not only elusive plants that thrive under the shade of beech trees, the thick layer of slowly decomposing leaf litter creates an ideal environment for a vast range of fungi. The beech plays host to more fungi than any other tree; many types of fungi grow alongside the tree roots in a symbiotic, mutually beneficial relationship. These fungi include prized truffles and, as a result, beech woodlands are playground to truffle hounds and their owners from late spring right through to winter.

Smooth, thin, grey bark, sometimes with horizontal etches cut into the wood. Beech wood is used for smoking food such as meat and fish, giving a mild, nutty, smoked flavour.

In autumn the beech masts – small triangular nuts protected by a spiky casing – fall from the trees. Beech masts are rich in protein and can be eaten as a nut, ground into flour or processed for their oil content.

Beech nuts, known as masts form inside spiney, four-sided shells, which open up as they turn brown.

Oval young leaves have fine hairs along the edges. The leaves are silky textured and mildly sour. They become more opaque and shinier as they age, turning copper in the autumn and producing spectacular colour before they fall.

Fagus sylvatica

BEECH

Beech nuts are high in protein and oils. Produced in huge quantities every few years, the nuts can be used as a flour, roasted, added to stuffings and salads, or even turned into a coffee substitute. Ground nuts release a highly prized oil which was produced in France and Britain back in the 1800s; it is now one of the most rare and delicious oils, but it is very easy to produce at home with a juicer or grinder.

TO PROCESS BEECH NUTS

- Basket full of beech nuts

Although you can safely nibble on a few raw beech nuts, they contain a toxin called saponin glycoside which should be removed before eating in any volume. This can be done by soaking and heating the nuts. The process of shelling, soaking, roasting and grinding may be long, but when there is an abundant beech-mast harvest it is well worth the effort to prepare the nuts for use as an ingredient in their own right or for further processing into oil.

1. Gather the nuts when the shells are brown, then peel away their brown shiny casing and rub the nuts with a towel to remove the brown papery covering. Place the shelled and cleaned beech nuts into a bowl of water and leave to soak for a couple of hours. Drain the nuts and place on kitchen roll to dry out.

2. Preheat the oven to 120°C, 250°F, gas mark ½. Roast the nuts for 15–20 minutes to release the oils and break down the glycoside. Once roasted you can eat the nuts and use them in a wide range of recipes – they are a good substitute for hazelnut, pecan and Brazil nuts.

3. The rich oil content can be extracted with a blender. Blend the nuts to a fine powder, then process to a smooth purée – effectively to create a nut butter. Decant the butter into a deep jar and place in the fridge. After a day the oils will separate from the solid butter; carefully pour through a muslin cloth to remove any solids and store in a sealed bottle in a cool dark place. Use as a special dressing on savoury and sweet dishes. (Beech oil used to be stored for up to ten years in buried pots.) Don't bin the nut butter; use it as a spread.

BEECH LEAF AND TRUFFLE OIL PASTA

Serves 4

- 450g ribbon-like egg pasta
- Olive oil
- 1 garlic clove
- 150ml single cream
- 50g beech leaves, washed and papery stalks removed
- Drizzle of truffle oil
- Salt and freshly ground black pepper

To serve:
- Truffle shavings
- Parmesan shavings
- Finely grated lemon zest

The first flush of leaves coincides with the growth of summer truffles, which often form amongst the roots of beech trees.

1. Cook the pasta according to the packet instructions. While it is cooking, warm the olive oil over a low heat in a wide saucepan and add the garlic clove, swirling it in the oil for 2 minutes. Remove the garlic and pour in the cream. Once heated through, add the washed beech leaves and cook until they have wilted. Stir in a tiny drizzle of truffle oil, or add more to suit your taste.

2. Season with salt and pepper, then stir in the drained pasta with a spoonful of the cooking water. Finish with truffle and Parmesan shavings and finely grated lemon zest.

BEECH LEAF AND MAPLE LIQUEUR

Makes 1 litre

- 1 litre good-quality vodka
- Enough young beech leaves to pack into a wide-necked 1-litre jar
- 250ml dark amber maple syrup

Beech trees grow alongside sugar maples in vast woodlands in North America. These trees form such thick shade with their canopies that they are often the final trees to grow in a woodland, as the lack of light prevents any other trees from growing. These areas have become known as climax woodlands. Before beech leaves lose their translucency in the spring and block out the light, they can be infused into gin, vodka, brandy or rum to make beautifully flavoured liqueurs. Traditionally the leaves in these drinks are only soaked for a few weeks, but leave them in the alcohol for a few months and you will create a drink that tastes like a tea made from the woods. Once sweetened with maple syrup, you can imagine being sat in the middle of a shady North American woodland, drinking in your surroundings.

1. In the spring, gather enough beech leaves to fill a 1-litre jar. Cover the leaves with vodka, seal the jar and place in a dark cupboard for 4 months. After this time, the spring-made drink will have transformed into something that tastes of the approaching autumnal season of mellow fruitfulness.

2. Strain the vodka and squeeze any excess from the leaves, then stir in as much dark maple syrup as you wish. Bottle and sup through the autumn.

LINDEN

Tilia spp.

❧ DISTRIBUTION

Native to most parts of
Europe, Asia and North
America.

❧ HABITAT

Ancient woodlands, parkland,
frequently planted in town
parks and streets.

**❧ GATHERING
SEASONS**

Early spring:
Sap.

Mid-spring:
Opening leaf buds and young
leaves.

Summer:
Freshly opened flowers and
leaves.

Autumn:
Seeds.

Walk along a tree-lined city street in high summer and you may be struck by the hum of bees and the heady, sweet melon perfume of cream flowers which hang with bow-like helicopters from the boughs of linden trees. All across the world, lindens are a town-planner's go-to tree to green even the most densely populated streets. Their large canopies create shade and capture carbon dioxide, cleaning and cooling the polluted city air, and offering a moment of green calm from the chaos of city life.

Linden trees also have a long association with villages and towns; across Slavic countries important civic meetings would take place under the sweeping boughs of linden trees, and symbolic moments such as the day on which Slovenia declared independence have been celebrated by the planting of a linden tree. And it's not just people who congregate under the trees; for a few weeks a year the boughs teem with thousands of bees collecting the sweetest of nectar from the flowers that bloom in the heat of summer. The perfumed flowers are dried to make a traditional tea with calming and healing properties. They have been used to soothe and heal convalescing patients over thousands of years, leading to the planting of lindens around hospitals, providing an easy-to-gather supply of the herbal tea, and turning hospital grounds into perfumed pharmacies.

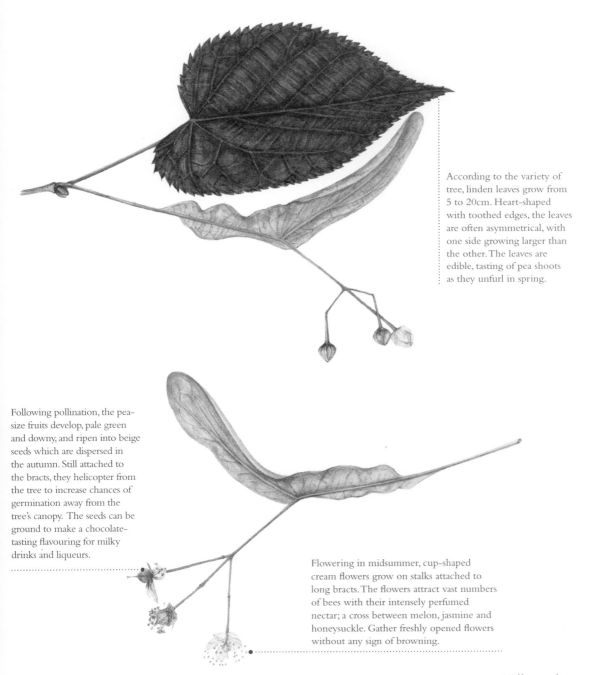

According to the variety of tree, linden leaves grow from 5 to 20cm. Heart-shaped with toothed edges, the leaves are often asymmetrical, with one side growing larger than the other. The leaves are edible, tasting of pea shoots as they unfurl in spring.

Following pollination, the pea-size fruits develop, pale green and downy, and ripen into beige seeds which are dispersed in the autumn. Still attached to the bracts, they helicopter from the tree to increase chances of germination away from the tree's canopy. The seeds can be ground to make a chocolate-tasting flavouring for milky drinks and liqueurs.

Flowering in midsummer, cup-shaped cream flowers grow on stalks attached to long bracts. The flowers attract vast numbers of bees with their intensely perfumed nectar; a cross between melon, jasmine and honeysuckle. Gather freshly opened flowers without any sign of browning.

Tillia cordata

LINDEN

Every part of the linden tree is edible. In early spring the trees can be tapped for their nutritious, mineral-rich sap. The young emerging leaf buds taste of sugar snap peas, and the young leaves, rich in antioxidants, flavonoids and vitamin C, are delicious added to salads. Older leaves can be dried and ground to make a grassy-tasting flour; linden leaves contain mucilage and can be used as a thickener in soups and stews.

LINDEN LEAF MADELEINES
Makes 12

- 120g plain flour, plus 1 tbsp to coat the tin
- 2 tsp dried linden leaves, finely ground to a powder
- 100g sugar
- 2 large free-range organic eggs
- 1 tsp vanilla extract
- Pinch of salt
- Zest of 1 lemon, 1 tbsp juice
- 110g butter, melted, plus 2 tbsp
- 12-hole madeleine or jam tart tin

The novelist Marcel Proust famously wrote about a madeleine cake evoking memories of his aunt dipping the little cakes into her linden tea. Linden leaf cakes might not take you back in time, but they will take you somewhere delicious.

1. Whisk together the flour, linden powder and sugar in a mixing bowl.

In another bowl, whisk the eggs, vanilla, salt, lemon juice and lemon zest until frothy. Add the eggs to the flour, stirring until just combined, followed by the melted butter. Continue to stir until the butter has blended with the batter; as soon as it does, stop stirring. Rest the batter in the fridge for at least an hour.

2. Mix 2 tablespoons of butter and 1 tablespoon of flour to a paste and use it to brush the tin shells, then place in a freezer for 30 minutes or until the butter paste has hardened.

3. Preheat the oven to 175°C, 325°F, gas mark 3.

4. Fill each of the frozen tin shells with 1 tablespoon of the chilled batter and cook for 10–12 minutes, until the cakes are puffed up and spring back when pressed. Cool and serve dipped in Linden tea (see opposite).

MELON, CUCUMBER, LINDEN AND MINT SALAD
Serves 4

- 2 firm cucumbers
- 1 cantaloupe melon, halved, seeds and skin removed
- 2 tsp dried linden flowers
- ½ tbsp lemon juice
- 2 tbsp olive oil
- 20g chives, finely chopped
- 20g mint leaves, finely chopped
- Pinch of salt
- Fresh linden flowers (if in season)
- Salted ricotta or Parma ham, to serve

Linden and mint are traditionally blended together to make a refreshing French herbal tea, '*tilleul menthe*'. Combined with melon, cucumber and mint, this easy-to-make salad would cool the most wilting of souls.

1. Purée 1 cucumber and half of the melon, then strain the pulp through a sieve and collect the juice in a jar. Add the dried linden flowers and leave the liquid to infuse for 1 hour. Strain, and whisk in the lemon juice, oil, chopped chives and mint and the salt.

2. Slice the remaining cucumber and melon flesh into thin slivers, coat with the dressing and garnish with fresh linden flowers, if you have them. Serve with salted ricotta or Parma ham.

LINDEN TEA
Makes 50g

- 250g newly opened linden flowers, bracts and leaves

Infusing freshly gathered linden flowers, bracts and leaves makes a beautiful, soothing, summertime tea. But linden tea is more than just a delicious drink; it contains compounds that reduce anxiety, act as antispasmodics and help to ease stomach cramps and headaches. The mucilage in the plant helps soothe coughs, while other compounds in it help reduce fevers. Drying the flowers, bracts and leaves for use later in the year provides a valuable herbal tea, which tastes every bit as delicious as when it is drunk fresh. Drying is a simple process, and this technique can be applied to different plants.

1. Gather freshly opened flowers and bracts on a sunny day, at least 24 hours after any rain. Try to gather before midday, when the flavour will be at its peak. Shake off any insects, and as soon as possible lay the flowers on a clean cloth in a dehydrator or layered on a wicker tray (a cooling rack will work just as well) and place in a warm, dry room away from direct sunshine. If drying on a tray, turn the flowers a few times each day. If after a day the flowers have not started to dry, place them in the oven on its lowest setting for an hour or until they are dry enough to crumble. Once completely dried out, store in an airtight jar in a dark cupboard for up to a year.

2. To make linden tea, use 1–2 teaspoons of dried linden per cup, pour over just-boiled water, cover and leave to steep for 10 minutes before drinking. Linden flower tea is safe for children and makes a soothing bedtime drink for both children and weary adults.

OAK

Quercus spp.

At least 600 varieties of oak tree grow across the world, adapted to different climates and ranging from scrubby, gnarled trees on hillsides to stately monuments in manicured parkland. Before we started eating grains and growing crops, the landscape was dominated by forests; and within them, vast numbers of oak trees – long-lived trees that provided some of the most important food in the world for both people and animals. Acorns are an incredibly nutritious, perfectly balanced package of carbohydrates and proteins, along with omega 3 fats, calcium, phosphorus, potassium, niacin and vitamin E. In a good year's harvest, forest floors were covered with acorns, which were gathered, stored, processed and baked on flat stones heated in fires. Even in years when acorns weren't plentiful, they provided nourishment. Oak trees don't produce large harvests each year but their rich tannic content that makes them too bitter to eat without processing acted as a preservative, which meant that dried nuts could be stored in their shells for years. In a good harvest, people would gather huge quantities of the nuts, burying them in pits like squirrels, to unearth in lean years.

We stopped eating acorns once we began cultivating grains, slowly changing our taste towards sweet, pale gluten-rich flours rather than the richer brown meal of tree nuts. Acorns and other nuts became known as starvation food, only returned to the table during times of famine, and are now seen as an ingredient of choice to only a few, the majority happily eating carbohydrates from farms rather than forests. But, scattered through farmland, scrubland and mountainsides, oak trees continue growing, asking for no effort from us, and make only a positive impact on the planet. Cleaning the air, nourishing the ground, supporting a wealth of biodiversity and producing highly abundant, storable and nutritious food without demanding water, ploughing, fertilizers or pesticides. Truly sustainable and exceptionally nutritious, perhaps the acorn could do with a rebrand?

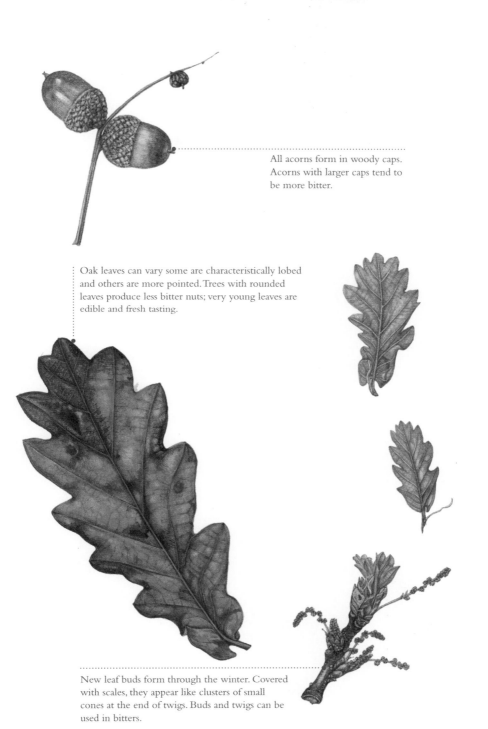

All acorns form in woody caps. Acorns with larger caps tend to be more bitter.

Oak leaves can vary some are characteristically lobed and others are more pointed. Trees with rounded leaves produce less bitter nuts; very young leaves are edible and fresh tasting.

New leaf buds form through the winter. Covered with scales, they appear like clusters of small cones at the end of twigs. Buds and twigs can be used in bitters.

Quercus petraea

OAK

All edible parts of Oak trees are rich in tannins; the young leaves make leaf wines and liqueurs, the budding twigs can be made into bitters (see page 15), and once the tannins have been extracted, the abundant acorns can be used in any recipe that calls for nuts or nut-based flour.

HOW TO PREPARE ACORNS

All acorns contain tannic acid, which make them very bitter and astringent. The tannins need to be removed before they are safe to eat and there are two ways to do this: hot and cold leaching. Hot leaching is better for very bitter nuts or nuts you plan to eat whole, but because it cooks the starches, hot-leached nuts are less suitable for use in baking.

1. First gather your nuts; only collect acorns without holes. Remove the acorns from their caps and place in a bucket of water, discard any that float to the top.

2. Remove the acorns from the water and spread them out on a tea towel somewhere warm to dry for a few days, until the shells become brittle and the nuts shrink enough to be able to hear them shaking inside the shells.

To **cold-leach**, crack the acorns out of the shells. Rub them with a tea towel to remove the brown papery skin. To make flour, grind the acorns in a food processor with three times more water than acorns until they have broken down into a rough purée. Strain and place in a large container, fill with water and leave to leach for a day before ladling off the water and refilling with fresh water. Repeat this process until the nut mixture has lost any bitter flavour. Strain and spread the pulp out on a clean cloth and dry in a warm place until powdery.

To **hot-leach**, place shelled whole or roughly chopped acorns in a pan of cold water, slowly bring it to a simmer, and keep the pan over a gentle heat until the water becomes dark, then scoop out the acorns and place in another pan of simmering water until this water also turns brown. Taste the nuts when you remove them from one pan, and as soon as they lose their bitterness, stop leaching. After drying the flour or nuts, store them in the fridge for up to a month or the freezer for a year.

KOREAN ACORN JELLY SALAD – DOTORI-MUK

Serves 4

- 60g acorn flour, ground to a fine powder
- 750ml water
- ½ tsp salt
- 100ml light soy sauce
- 1 tsp rice wine vinegar
- 1 tbsp honey or sugar
- ½ tsp chilli flakes
- 3 garlic cloves, grated
- 1 tsp sesame oil
- 1 cucumber, finely sliced
- 1 carrot, finely sliced
- 2 spring onions, finely sliced
- A bunch of fresh coriander (or perilla)
- 1 tbsp toasted sesame seeds
- Kimchi, to serve

Acorn jelly is a Korean speciality. It is usually made into a savoury jelly, but by adding honey or sugar to the flour and water mixture, along with warming spices, the jelly can also be made into a sweet dessert.

1. In a bowl, mix together the acorn flour, water and salt, stirring until smooth. Pour the mixture into a heavy-based pan and place on a medium heat, stirring continuously until it starts to bubble. Turn the heat right down and stir until the mixture is thickened. Pour into a flat-bottomed dish and leave to cool before putting into the fridge, to chill for a few hours until solid.

2. Turn the jelly onto a chopping board and cut into slivers. Whisk together the soy, vinegar, honey or sugar, chilli flakes, garlic and sesame oil. Lightly cover the jelly in the dressing and toss in the cucumber, carrot, spring onions, coriander and sesame seeds and serve with kimchi.

SALTED ACORN PRALINE

Makes 200g

- 200g hard butterscotch sweets
- Oil, for greasing
- 100g shelled hot-leached acorns, chipped or whole
- Pinch of sea salt

After all the effort of processing, you deserve an easy recipe to make the most of your finds. If you are not a butterscotch fan, hot-leached acorns are also delicious just ground into salt, with a pinch of sugar added as a sweetly salty seasoning.

1. Preheat the oven to 120°C, 250°F, gas mark ½.

2. Grind the sweets into crumbs, then scatter over oiled baking paper on a baking tray. Roll the acorns in the sweet mixture, ensuring they are fully covered, sprinkle with a pinch of salt, and place in the oven. When the butterscotch crumbs soften and adhere to the acorns, remove from the oven and leave to cool.

3. Once cold, break into pieces and store in an airtight container. You can also grind the mixture into a coarse powder to sprinkle on ice creams, cakes and chocolates.

DAMSON

Prunus insititia

❧ DISTRIBUTION

Native to Europe and Asia,
introduced to America and
Australia.

❧ HABITAT

Woodland edges, hedges,
gardens and orchards.

**❧ GATHERING
SEASONS**

Early spring:
Blossom, leaves.

Late summer–early autumn:
Fruit.

Damsons belong to a group of plum trees known as Prunus, a group of trees that includes astringent sloes, bullace and sweeter cherry plums. The oval fruits of damsons droop from hedgerows and small scrubby trees in late summer and early autumn. Their flavours range from sweet enough to eat from the tree, to so sour they can make your face contort – not much sweeter than a mouthful of sloe berries. There is a good reason that damsons can taste so similar to sloes, as it is thought that they originated from a cross-pollination of the lip-puckering fruit and their sweeter relative, the cherry plum. Damson's exact origins genetically and geographically have been cause for disagreement for many years – right back to the era of the Roman Empire, when writers named the fruit 'damson' after its supposed origins in Damascus, because it grew in abundance in the region.

Wherever damsons originated from, their sour, fruity appeal has been long enjoyed. Before our taste turned saccharine, damsons were used in both savoury and sweet dishes, from gamey meats to floral-infused desserts. Damsons provided a fruit rich in dietary fibre, copper, iron and anthocyanin-rich antioxidants. During the eighteenth century, the British used enslaved people to work on sugar plantations in the West Indies in order to export cheap sugar. This led to diets changing and damsons being sweetened; huge amounts of conserves were produced to feed the new sugar addiction. British troops in World War I were sent out with tins of sweet damson jam to boost energy and morale. As sugar became more widely consumed, so our appetite for sour tastes diminished and the sometimes-sweet, sometimes-sour damson fell out of favour. Over the next decades, vast numbers of vibrant damson orchards were neglected and often dug up. But fortunes are changing again for the purple plum, and now the lesser-spotted damson trees are sought-after once more, championed by chefs and campaigners for traditional fruit and sourer flavours. Damsons have made their mark once again on the culinary landscape, dying aprons and work surfaces throughout the autumn.

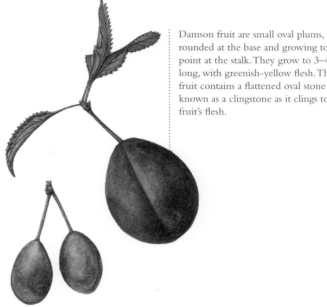

Damson fruit are small oval plums, rounded at the base and growing to a point at the stalk. They grow to 3–4cm long, with greenish-yellow flesh. The fruit contains a flattened oval stone known as a clingstone as it clings to the fruit's flesh.

Small white flowers with a subtle almond scent appear in clusters of two or three just as the leaves start to open. The blossom can be candied or used in liqueurs and syrups, giving a delicate almond flavour.

Small and oval, with a rounded end, pointed at the stalk, the leaves mirror the shape of the fruit. The leaves are toothed, with pairs of indents forming a pattern around the edges. Young leaves can be infused into liqueurs (see page 64).

DAMSON

The tart, astringent, bitter skins of the fruit may make damsons challenging to eat raw but this makes them incredibly versatile in both sweet and savoury dishes. From Roman recipes using the fruit as a sauce for venison, to sixteenth-century damson-laced chicken pies, damsons are great partners for game and poultry dishes. Their intense flavour makes them a superb fruit to preserve, either as jam, fruit cheese or whole in syrups, pickles or fruit liqueurs.

OVEN-ROASTED DAMSON AND ROSE PETAL PRESERVE
Makes 500g

- 1kg damsons, washed
- 250g unrefined sugar
- 1 cup scented rose petals cut into grass-like slithers (or 1 tsp of rose water)

Slowly cooking damsons in the oven slightly dehydrates the fruit, concentrating the natural sugars. Roasted damsons were steeped in rose water in sixteenth-century recipes, and rose petals mellow the intensity of the damson's flavour.

1. Preheat the oven to 75°C, 165°F, gas mark ¼.

2. Place the damsons on a baking tray and cook in the oven for 2 hours, then remove and press out the stones, which should leave the fruit cleanly now the flesh is soft. Put the damson flesh in a bowl and stir in the sugar and rose petals or water, ensuring the petals are covered by the pulp. Return to the oven and continue cooking, stirring occasionally, until the mixture has dehydrated and thickened.

3. Pour into sterilized jars and pasteurize (see page 9 for details) before storing. Serve with yoghurt, in baked ricotta pies or with ice cream.

DAMSON AND HONEYSUCKLE SOURS
Makes 2 drinks

- 500g sour damsons, washed (to make damson juice)
- 100ml dry apple juice
- A handful of honeysuckle flowers or a few smashed cardamom seeds
- 2 tsp sugar syrup or Honeysuckle cordial (see page 77)
- 1 egg white
- A few ice cubes

Damson juice can be used in place of lemons in cocktails, turning Sours into something far more interesting and vibrant than the sum of their original parts. However, drinkers of alcohol shouldn't have all the fun, and this guilt-free cocktail is wincingly delicious. Use fresh honeysuckle if you can find any twisting through your damson tree, or a few smashed cardamom seeds.

1. Place the damsons in a pan with a cup of water and cook over a low heat until the juices have come out of the fruit. Strain (reserving the softened fruit for jams or compotes) into a bowl, cover and keep the juice in the fridge or freezer until needed.

2. When ready to serve, add all the ingredients to a shaker with ice and shake, then strain and serve in a coupe or martini glass with a honeysuckle flower to decorate.

PICKLED DAMSONS
Makes 1kg

- 500g sugar
- 1 cinnamon stick
- 3 cloves
- 2 tsp allspice berries
- 2cm piece of fresh root ginger, peeled
- 600ml cider vinegar
- 1kg damsons, washed and pricked with a needle

Pickled damsons are sensational served with roast vegetables or meats, smoked meats and cheeses. The liquid from the damsons is like a sticky balsamic and every drizzle of it should be devoured.

1. Heat the sugar, spices and vinegar in a pan over a medium heat, stirring until the sugar has dissolved, then pour this over the pricked damsons in a heatproof bowl. Cover and leave in the fridge overnight.

2. Strain the pickling liquid into a pan, bring it to a boil and reduce until it starts to thicken slightly (but not caramelize). Place the damsons into sterilized jars and cover with the hot, syrupy vinegar. Leave to mature for 3–4 weeks before using.

HAZEL

Corylus spp.

❧ DISTRIBUTION

Native to Asia and Europe
and naturalized in many parts
of the temperate world.

❧ HABITAT

A common tree in ancient
woodlands, planted in hedges,
riverbanks and margins.

**❧ GATHERING
SEASONS**

Winter:
Catkins.

Spring–summer:
Young leaves.

Late summer/early autumn:
Nuts.

A shrubby member of the pioneering birch family, hazels were
thought to be amongst the first trees to re-establish themselves on
barren lands as the last Ice Age thawed. Aided by returning people
and nut-caching animals such as squirrels and mice, the fruits of hazel
trees were carried from one location to another. Buried and forgotten
about, new saplings could germinate and groves of hazel trees soon
formed. The slim branches of hazel were ideal for producing straight
poles for thatching, wattle and daub and making homes.

Just as hazel provided shelter, so it also provided nourishment – across
Europe archaeological digs have discovered numerous hazelnut-
processing sites dating back thousands of years; pits of burnt, opened
hazelnut shells, the discard of roasting significant amounts of nuts,
an important source of energy in the pre-grain era. Whether people
who roasted and cracked open the nuts did so for flavour is unknown,
but roasted hazelnuts are sweeter, 'nuttier' and more flavoursome
than those eaten raw. Not only does roasting enhance the flavour, but
drying out the excess moisture helps create a crop that can be stored;
and with an oil content of up to 60 per cent, hazelnuts provide a vital
supply of fats for the lean winter months. Hazelnuts are also laden
with protein and minerals, including beneficial fatty acids, vitamin E,
calcium, magnesium, iron, phosphorous and potassium – perfect to
sustain the hungriest of squirrels and people.

Corylus avellana

Hazel leaves are oval to round with pointed tips and toothed edges. The leaf is creased from the central vein, the underside of hazel leaves are hairy, as are the leaf stems. Hazel leaves are rich in antioxidants and are used in herbal medicines and teas. Edible, slightly bitter, pollen-filled catkins form during the winter alongside tiny red star-shaped flowers.

Growing in groups of up to four fruit, often at the end of branches, the fruit are held on the tree as they grow by cup-shaped leaves (known as bracts). The nuts can be harvested once the flesh has filled the shell – the shell of ripening nuts starts to develop pinkish tinges before turning brown. Fresh, creamy nuts are a late-summer delicacy in sweet and savoury dishes, but only ripe hazelnuts will store for any length of time.

45

HAZEL

Hazelnuts are still an important part of diets across the world, but most of our consumption of the nut is now in conjunction with chocolate; nearly 90 per cent of the world's cultivated hazelnuts are used to make pralines and chocolate spreads. Though chocolate and hazelnuts make a delicious pair, so too do hazelnuts and pears, ginger, cheese and bitter vegetables.

KENTISH COBNUT CAKE

Makes 8 slices

- 50g fresh hazelnuts
- 225g self-raising flour
- 1 rounded tsp ground ginger
- 110g butter, at room temperature
- 110g light brown sugar
- 2 medium eggs, beaten

Hazelnuts gathered in late summer are often milky and uniquely flavoured. Sold as a speciality crop across Britain, green hazelnuts are beautiful served in seasonal salads, but roasting them gently turns them into the most delicious sweet nut. This recipe hails from Kent, where cultivated forms of hazelnuts known as cobnuts are grown in nut groves.

1. Preheat the oven to 120°C, 250°F, gas mark ½. Place the nuts on a baking sheet and roast in the oven until golden – how long depends on their size and how dry they are, so check on them as they cook. Remove from the oven and leave to cool. Once cool, pulse in a food processor to make a coarse flour.

2. Turn the oven up to 165°C, 325°F, gas mark 3, and grease and line a 23 × 10cm loaf tin with baking paper.

3. Sift the self-raising flour into a mixing bowl with the ginger and rub in the butter until the mixture looks like breadcrumbs. Gently mix in the sugar and ground nuts. Finally, stir in the beaten eggs – the mixture should be dry and crumbly; if you overwork it it'll become like a dense biscuit mixture and won't be such a crumbly cake. Spoon the mixture into your tin, press down gently, but do not compact the mixture. Cook for 20–30 minutes until it's crunchy looking on top but slightly claggy inside.

4. This very wet cake is delicious served with whipped cream or eaten fresh from the cooling rack, with butter and brown sugar.

HAZELNUT TARATOR SAUCE

Makes around 350g

....

- 100g hazelnuts, blanched to remove their skins
- 75g breadcrumbs (white or brown)
- 2 garlic cloves
- 175ml olive oil
- 80ml white wine vinegar
- ½ tsp salt

....

Tarator sauces are familiar all over the eastern Mediterranean; creamy condiments that can be served with fish, meats or vegetables. In Turkey, where most of the world's hazelnut production comes from, tarator sauce is often made with nuts including hazelnuts.

1. Pulse the nuts in a food processor or grinder until finely ground, but not turning into a paste. Add the breadcrumbs, garlic and a splash of water. If you are using a processor, keep it running whilst slowly pouring in the olive oil, followed by the vinegar, and blend until smooth. Finally, add the salt. (You can also use a pestle and mortar, which will give a more textured, less smooth sauce.)

2. Transfer to a serving bowl, cover and chill the sauce until needed.

CHOCOLATE-COVERED HAZELNUTS

Makes a bag of 20

....

- 20 shelled hazelnuts
- 150g dark chocolate
- 2 tsp nut or fruit liqueur (optional)
- Cocoa powder, for dusting

....

Chocolate-covered hazelnuts can be made with either fresh or ripened nuts, they just need to be roasted before use. This recipe works best with whole kernels; cracking nuts by holding the top and bottom of the shell with the nut cracker helps keep the nuts whole.

1. Preheat the oven to 120°C, 250°F, gas mark ½. Place the hazelnuts on a baking sheet and roast in the oven until nutty brown and hardened – how long depends on their size and how dry they are, so check on them as they cook.

2. Break the chocolate into a heatproof bowl and set over a pan of simmering water, or in a bain-marie. Heat until the chocolate has started to melt and, if using, stir in the liqueur. Push a clean pin into the top of a hazelnut and swirl it in the chocolate mix until it is covered with a good layer of chocolate. Place the chocolate-covered nut on a dish dusted with cocoa powder and roll it in the powder until covered. Repeat with all the nuts.

3. Leave the nuts to harden, and store in a sealed container until you are ready to eat them or, although unlikely, give them away.

Oval leaves with toothed edges, growing up to 5–6cm in length, which open after the blossom. Domestic apple leaves are downy, crab apple leaves tend to be less so, often with no hairiness. Crab apple leaves, along with the inner bark, are used to make herbal teas in China.

Bright pink buds open up to reveal five-petalled, sweetly scented, pale pink blossom growing in clusters along the leaf stems. Blossoms have a grapefruit flavour with a rose-petal-like texture and can be gathered when in bud or when fully open.

There are over 40 species of crab apple trees and their fruit can vary widely, from tiny red or orange oval apples on long stalks to yellow-green fruit that look like small cultivated apples. All apples have five seed chambers (carpels), which give a star-shaped appearance to the centre of an apple if you slice it open across the middle.

Malus sylvestris

CRAB APPLE

Malus spp.

DISTRIBUTION

Native to Europe, Asia and
North America. Introduced
to New Zealand and
Australia.

HABITAT

Woodland margins, wood
pastures, hedgerows,
scrubland and frequently
planted in orchards.

**GATHERING
SEASONS**

Spring:
Blossoms and young leaves.

Late summer–early winter:
Fruit.

Dotted through apple orchards you will often find crab apple trees planted as pollinating partners for the domesticated crop. The wild apple's long flowering season, and blossoms that are laden with far more pollen than their domestic relatives, help ensure that harvests of cultivated apples are abundant enough to fulfil the world's demand for the sweet fruit. Not only do crab apples help produce the most commonly eaten of fruits, they also act as a sour reminder of the fruit's family tree. All of the sweet apples we eat today have had their ancestries traced to a marriage of wild apples, including the European native wild crab apple, *Malus sylvestris* and wild sweet apples that originated in the foothills of the Tian Shan mountain range in Central Asia (known as *Malus sieversii*). Originally the sweet apples of Tian Shan were moved by giant megafauna who gorged on the fallen fruit, depositing the seeds as they roamed from place to place. Once the giant beasts disappeared, people took on the role of taking the fruit further from its homelands, propagating, planting and tending the trees further and further from the mountain range, until the pollen-laden blossoms of *Malus sieversii* were close enough to those of native European crab apples for flying insects to cross-pollinate the two species, contributing to the creation of *Malus domestica*, the apples we eat today.

So successful has been the establishment of cultivated apples, that the chances are that if you find an apple growing wild, you have most likely found an escaped domestic variety, the seed dropped by a bird or thrown out of the window of a moving car in a chewed apple core. There are now very few true wild crab apple trees, but you can still find them in woodlands and growing in 'wood pastures' – lush pastureland filled with ancient trees and grazing livestock. Should you stumble upon a proper crab apple tree in the wild, cut off a few twigs after the tree has blossomed and try propagating a new crab apple tree, helping to keep the ancestors of the fruit in most of our shopping baskets alive.

CRAB APPLE

Crab apples vary in taste, just as cultivated apples do. Before you gather from a newly found tree, take a bite from your apple – some taste acrid and it is better not to waste hours gathering the fruit to discover they are unpalatable. But find a sour, intensely fruity crab apple and it will offer an array of culinary opportunities.

Crab apples that break down and become fluffy when cooked are traditionally added to a British midwinter wassail drink known as Lambswool, ceremonially served to celebrate the apple harvest. In China the fruit is sugared and preserved and then served to wish prosperity to couples at their wedding, and the apples and leaves are dried and used in fruity herbal teas. Crab apples also make exceptional preserves, including the very best jellies; sour and pectin-rich, they pair beautifully with other hedgerow fruit, flowers and herbs.

ROASTED CRAB APPLES
Serves 4

- 500g small crab apples
- 1 tsp ground cinnamon
- 1 tsp sugar (optional)

Slowly roasting crab apples intensifies both the flavour and sweetness of the fruit, turning them from wincingly sour to sweet and soft enough to graze on; the slow roasting even softens the core and pips of small crab apples so they can be eaten in one mouthful. Delicious served with roast goose or pork or simply eaten by themselves.

1. Preheat the oven to 100°C, 200°F, gas mark ¼.

2. Lay the crab apples on a large sheet of baking paper, dust with cinnamon and, if you wish, sugar. Make a parcel with the baking paper, making sure the fruit is sealed inside before wrapping the parcel in tin foil. Place in the oven for 2 hours, until the apples are soft enough to eat whole.

APPLE BLOSSOM MARTINI

Makes 4 cocktails

- Enough apple blossom to pack a 250g jar (reserve some to garnish)
- 220ml delicately flavoured gin
- 110ml sweet vermouth
- 110ml apple juice
- A grating of zest from an unwaxed grapefruit

Apple blossoms hold a grapefruit flavour in them. When they are in bud they can be preserved in salts or pickles just like cherry blossom (see page 19). Once the flowers have been pollinated, the apple blossom will start to fall off the tree: hold a bag or basket under the branches of apple blossoms and gently shake or touch the flowers; the blossom will fall into your basket to use in salads, in syrups or suspended in grown-up jellies. Turning them into an apple-themed martini is also a fitting farewell to the falling blossoms.

1. Pack a jar with blossoms and cover them with a good quality gin. Press the petals under the liquid and cover with baking paper to ensure that they do not come up to the surface. Seal with a lid and place in a dark cupboard to infuse for 3–4 hours before straining.

2. In a cocktail shaker, shake the gin, vermouth and apple juice with ice. Pour into chilled martini glasses, rub the rim with the grapefruit zest, and garnish the drink with the zest and reserved apple blossoms. Find a billowing apple tree to sit under, sipping your drink as blossoms fall all around you.

CRAB APPLE AIOLI

Makes 500g

- 200g crab apples
- 4 egg yolks
- 2 garlic cloves, crushed
- 500ml extra virgin olive oil
- Salt and sugar, to taste

The pulp left over from cooking crab apples for jelly-making is beautiful turned into numerous preserves, including fruit cheeses or leathers, and when blended into an aioli it makes an incredibly flavoured, deeply savoury condiment. (If you want to make it without eggs, simply add more apple purée.)

1. Place the crab apples in a pan and cover with water, then cook over a medium heat until the apples are falling apart. (How long this takes depends on your apple variety, so check regularly, adding more water if required.) Strain the apples through a sieve set over a bowl to catch the pectin-rich liquid (this can be used to make jellies or in drinks). Then, over a clean bowl, press the cooked apples through a sieve to capture the smooth pulp.

2. Blend the yolks in a food processor with the garlic and apple pulp. Keeping the processor running, add the oil to the apple mixture in a slow stream until it is emulsified. Season with salt, adding a small amount of sugar if the aioli is too sour.

CHESTNUT

Castanea spp.

❦ DISTRIBUTION

Native to temperate regions
of the Northern Hemisphere,
now growing in all temperate
regions of the world.

❦ HABITAT

Well-drained moist
woodlands, often found on
sloping deep soils at the edge
of woodlands.

**❦ GATHERING
SEASONS**

Autumn:
Ripe chestnuts, usually
gathered from the ground or
plucked from low-hanging
branches.

Chestnuts have grown across the world for millions of years. Their
rot-resistant strong wood and abundant carbohydrate-rich nuts led
them to become one of the most-valued trees in Asia, Europe and
America. Each continent has its own native species of chestnut, and
each species evolved to thrive in its own environment; the trees
covered large swathes of the landmass of the globe. The nutritional
value of chestnuts led to them being taken across lands by people;
as the Roman Empire expanded, so chestnut groves were planted
across Europe and Britain. Chestnuts growing near Hadrian's Wall are
as much of a mark of Roman influence as the stones that span the
North of England.

This literal journey of the chestnut has led to much of its success,
but for one species our desire to move these nuts led to its downfall.
Up until the twentieth century, an estimated four billion American
chestnuts grew across the States, the East Coast almost blanketed by
the native tree. Fast-growing, wide and majestic, the tree produced
vast amounts of very sweet and nutty chestnuts that had been eaten
for thousands of years. But at the turn of the twentieth century an
Asian chestnut, with its captivatingly larger fruit, was imported to the
States, unknowingly bringing with it a fungus that attacked the bark
of the vulnerable American chestnut tree, killing mature chestnuts in
their billions. By the 1950s the native American chestnut was all but
extinct, and the American landscape was forever changed. Ironically,
the chestnuts that roast on open fires across America are now usually
imported from Asia, just as the fungus was.

The large oblong leaves are pointed at the end and feature numerous pairs of veins extending from the middle of the leaf. In summer, chestnut trees are easily spotted because they can be covered with catkins at least 20cm long, which can be seen even from a distance.

Chestnuts are large, long-lived trees, growing up to 35 metres high with a grey smooth bark that becomes marked with net-shaped splits as the trees age.

Caution: Do not confuse chestnut with horse chestnut. Chestnut leaves are pointed and the shells densely covered in sharp prickles; horse chestnut leaves are more rounded, and the spines on the fruit are wider apart, squatter and more rubbery.

Following summer flowering, brown shiny nuts form inside spiny cases; ripening in mid-autumn, the shells and nuts can cover the ground underneath chestnut trees. Gather the nuts by stamping on the shells to open them, and wear gardening gloves to extract them. Unique to these nuts, the chestnut fruit has a carbohydrate composition that is like grain.

Castanea sativa

CHESTNUT

Chestnuts have been eaten for thousands of years; long before grains were cultivated, chestnuts provided an important form of carbohydrate – the flesh of the chestnut is unique in its similarity to grain carbohydrates, which perhaps explains its popularity as a gluten-free flour. Chestnut flour is made into bread, pasta and polenta, with a mild but delicious sweetness; known as 'sweet flour' by Italians it is often used in cakes.

BRAISED CHICKEN WITH CHESTNUTS
Serves 4

- 8 chicken thighs
- 2 tbsp light soy sauce
- 2 tbsp vegetable oil
- Thumb-sized piece of fresh root ginger, grated
- 2 garlic cloves, finely chopped
- 6 shallots, finely diced
- 1 tbsp rice wine
- 250g shelled chestnuts
- 2 star anise
- 1 tbsp dark soy sauce
- ½ tsp salt
- 1 tbsp sesame oil
- 2 spring onions, finely chopped, to serve

This dish is inspired by Sichuanese recipes, and is made with the chestnuts that grow wild across the region.

1. Place the chicken thighs in a pan of boiling water to cook for 1 minute, then remove from the heat, drain, transfer to a bowl and marinate in the light soy sauce for 15 minutes.

2. Heat the oil in a wok. Add the chicken and brown it on both sides. Add the ginger, garlic and shallots and sweat until translucent and the shallots are softening. Add enough water to completely cover the chicken, then let it slowly simmer for 10 minutes. Add all the other ingredients except the sesame oil and spring onions and simmer for 15–20 minutes or until the chestnuts are softened. Then remove the chicken and chestnuts to a serving dish and increase the heat to reduce the sauce to a thick consistency.

3. When thickened, add the sesame oil and pour the sauce over the chicken and chestnuts, garnishing with the spring onions.

CHESTNUT CANTUCCI

Makes around 20 biscuits

- 3 free-range organic eggs
- 80g soft brown sugar
- 100g plain flour
- 250g chestnut flour
- 1 tsp baking powder
- 2–3 tbsp full-fat milk
- 100g hazelnuts

Cantucci biscuits are a Tuscan delicacy – twice-baked biscuits that are traditionally dunked in dessert wine. Chestnut flour in breads and baking is now known as a regional delicacy; however the idea comes from a time when wheat was too expensive to use but chestnuts were abundant. Chestnut flour is now vastly more expensive than wheat flour, but you can make your own by drying out chestnuts in a dehydrator or very low oven until they are hard before grinding them in a food processor until powdered.

1. Preheat the oven to 150°C, 300°F, gas mark 2 and line a large baking tray with baking paper.

2. Whisk the eggs in a large bowl with the sugar until doubled in volume. Sift in the plain and chestnut flours with the baking powder, then add enough milk to form a workable dough, folding in the hazelnuts, and shape the dough into a fat sausage, then bake for 30 minutes.

3. Remove from the oven, cut the log on a slant into 2cm-thick slices, then place them cut-side down on the baking paper and cook again for another 10–15 minutes or until crisped. Transfer to a wire rack to cool before serving.

VANILLA MARRONS GLACÉS

Makes around 500g

- 300g sugar
- 500g chestnuts, blanched and peeled
- 1 vanilla pod

Candied chestnuts were originally made in the Ottoman Empire, and soon they became popular in many chestnut-producing countries. French marrons glacés are regarded as the best candied chestnuts, and with the addition of vanilla they make beautiful sweet gifts for Christmas.

1. Heat the sugar and 300ml water in a pan until boiling, then cook, stirring, for a minute or two until the sugar has dissolved and the mixture has become syrupy. Add the chestnuts and vanilla pod, simmer for 7–8 minutes, then remove from the heat, cover and leave overnight at room temperature to infuse.

2. The following day, remove the vanilla pod, then bring the chestnuts and syrup back to the boil for 1 minute, then set aside to cool. Repeat this process over the next three or four days until all of the syrup has been absorbed by the chestnuts.

3. Dry out the chestnuts in an oven heated to 70°C, 160°F, gas mark ¼, until the sugars on the outside of the chestnuts is crystallized.

SHRUBS & CLIMBERS

Shrubs range from tiny mounds of ankle-skimming wild
blueberries to large, ancient elders and sea buckthorn which,
left unpruned, can grow into small trees. Shrubs are usually
the plants that form the hedgerows and thickets which
climbers scramble through, forming twisting, vine- and bine-
wrapped larders of fruit, nuts and edible flowers.

GORSE

Ulex spp.

DISTRIBUTION

Native to Europe, now present in all temperate regions of the world.

HABITAT

Dry, acidic soils – wind tolerant, found on commons, heathland, roadsides and coastal areas.

GATHERING SEASONS

Late winter–mid-spring:
Flowers.

All year:
Leaves and some species in flower.

The intoxicating coconut and vanilla perfume of gorse flowers sweetens the start of spring; sun-yellow-covered shrubs transform early spring heathlands and sand dunes long before other plants wake up and fill the landscape with colour. It's a well-timed early riser, the scent and colour drawing hungry bees for a spring feast. Little wonder gorse was used as a sacred plant in celebrations of festivals such as Beltane, marking the arrival of warmer days filled with sunshine as yellow as the flower.

On a warm spring day, stumbling across a gorse shrub is a delight, but once the flowers have turned to brown seed the plant loses its appeal; the rest of the landscape now awoken and filled with colour, gorse's glow replaced with a spiny dull thicket.

Devoid of its sunburst yellow and perfume, gorse suddenly looks like a menace rather than treasure, and is regarded in many countries as a noxious invasive weed. However, it was originally taken all over the world for its usefulness – gorse's fast-spreading nature only became clear when we stopped taking advantage of its many uses. Once widely used and valued, the shrubs were cut back and managed, the leaves and stems providing livestock with food, the dense oil-rich wood a valuable fuel source to heat ovens and homes, even the ash from gorse fires was used in soaps and as a potassium-rich source of fertilizer. Where gorse grew it did more than provide heat, fertilizer and feed – often growing in nutritionally depleted soil, gorse's nitrogen-fixing legume family roots spread far and wide, increasing the fertility of even the poorest of soils. Gorse's spreading roots also helped provide stability for loose soils, preventing erosion even on sandy ground. So valued was gorse that acts were passed in Britain to prevent overharvesting the shrub – a fuel, a food and a soil fixer. Gorse's beauty isn't only in the scented spring welcome, it turns out it lies in its summer spikes as well.

Ulex gallii

Gorse has pea-like pods filled with black seeds. These pods are a nod to gorse's membership of the pea family. Once the seeds are ripe, you can hear the pods bursting open like the crackling of rifles, firing the seeds metres away from the original plant. (The seeds and pods are inedible.)

Gorse is covered in sharp green spines; young gorse growth is initially tender but swiftly becomes hard. Seedlings have clover-shaped leaves which disappear as the plant matures. In the Mediterranean, branches and spines are used as aromatic flavourings.

Caution: Gorse contains small amounts of alkaloids, so while it is safe to eat small amounts of flowers, do not gorge on the plant.

You can find gorse in flower throughout the year, but you'll be looking at one of the three main species of gorse, which all live in different habitats and flower in different months. Gorse flowers from winter until late spring, with its big show happening in early spring. The heat of the sun warms the oils within the flowers that release a honeyed coconut scent.

GORSE

There is a rich, honey-flavoured history of using gorse in food, from the flowers perfuming whiskey in Ireland to branches of the shrub flavouring roast meats and rice dishes in Iberia. Gorse's flavours can be used in sweet and savoury dishes. Infused into chocolate, rum, lemonade and ice creams the sweet coconut flavour blossoms, but in salads, vinegars and oils, more savoury pea flavours dominate.

GORSE CHOCOLATE TRUFFLES
Makes 20 truffles

- 500-ml container of gorse flowers, freshly collected on a warm and sunny day
- 35g butter
- 200ml double cream
- 1 tbsp honey
- 200g good-quality dark chocolate (70% cocoa solids)

Cream and chocolate are ideal for capturing the flavour of gorse flowers.

1. Lay half the gorse flowers on a clean cloth and place in a dehydrator or on a warm radiator until dried out.

2. Heat the butter, cream and honey in a pan until the butter has melted, take off the heat and stir in the remaining gorse flowers. Cover, leave to cool, then refrigerate overnight.

3. Break the chocolate into a heatproof glass bowl. Place the pan of cream mixture on a low heat and warm through until the mixture is steaming hot. Place a sieve over the bowl of chocolate and pour the creamy liquid through it, discarding the spent flowers. Stir the ingredients vigorously until the chocolate has melted and you have a smooth ganache. Pour into a bowl, cover and place in a fridge for 4 hours.

4. Using a coffee or spice grinder, finely grind the dried gorse flowers and place in a bowl. Spoon out walnut-sized balls of the firmed-up chocolate mixture, moulding them in your hands before rolling them in the dried gorse flowers. Keep in the fridge for up to 5 days.

GORSE WITH RICE – CARQUEJA RICE

Serves 4

- 2 × 20cm lengths of dried gorse stems, gathered in flower
- 1 large onion, finely diced
- 2 garlic cloves
- Olive oil or lard, for frying
- 200g short grain rice, such as arborio
- Salt

In the Iberian region of the Mediterranean, gorse flowers and young shoots are dried for teas, petals are distilled into gins and whole stems used as herbs to flavour roast meats, fish and vegetables. In Portugal, stems of gorse are dried and infused into stocks to season game meats such as rabbit or hare. Carqueja rice is traditionally served with chicken but is equally delicious with grilled vegetables or bean stews.

1. Put the gorse stems in a jar with 1 litre of hot water and leave to infuse for at least 3 hours or overnight.

2. The next day, sweat the onion and garlic in a wide frying pan with a little olive oil or lard, then add the rice and cook until it is translucent. Slowly add the gorse-infused water and stir, then cover and cook for 20 minutes or until tender.

GORSE FLOWER SYRUP

Makes 500ml

- 500g unrefined sugar
- 1-litre jar of gorse flowers
- Juice of 1 lemon and/or 1 orange

Although the tropical coconut aroma of gorse hits you around the nose on a warm day, there are other perfumes in gorse flowers – earthy, herbal and fresh pea scents that might be hidden but shine when flowers are added to sweet flavours. Gorse flower syrup has enough coconut hints to it to be used with rum in wild piña coladas, but also enough honey to be at home drizzled on crumpets on chillier days. Gather your gorse flowers on a bright morning, gathering from the side of the shrub warmed by the sun, and you'll capture all the flavours that the bees love.

1. In a wide heavy-based pan, heat 400ml water and add the sugar. Bring to a rolling boil and keep boiling until the sugar has dissolved, stirring occasionally, and the mixture has become clear. Take the syrup off the heat immediately and leave to cool for 10 minutes, until cool enough to touch but still hot. Pour the syrup over the gorse flowers in the jar, cover with baking paper and push all the flowers down into the syrup to prevent oxidization, which spoils the flavour. Leave to infuse overnight.

2. The next day, strain the flowers through a fine cloth set in a sieve. (The sticky petals can be used in baking or dehydrated and ground into gorse sugar.) Taste the syrup, adding small amounts of citrus juice until you have a sweet, honeyed syrup with a hint of acidity – enough to stop the sugar from feeling cloying in your mouth. Bottle and store in the fridge until you can find some rum.

BLACKTHORN

Prunus spinosa

❧ DISTRIBUTION

Native to Europe, west
Asia and northwest Africa,
now naturalized in New
Zealand, Tasmania and North
America.

❧ HABITAT

Blackthorn grows in moist
soils in full sunshine or
dappled shade, as a bush or
small tree in forest margins,
scrubland and in planted
hedgerows.

**❧ GATHERING
SEASONS**

Early spring:
Freshly opened blossom.

Early–mid-spring:
Young, tender, almond-
scented leaves.

Mid–late autumn:
Berries.

The spines of blackthorn make it a prized hedging plant that forms impenetrable thickets which are often trimmed during annual hedge-cutting, but when left to its own devices the shrub grows into small trees, up to 5 metres high. These burst into flower early in spring, providing vital sources of nectar and pollen for bees in the flower-scarce months, but the almond-scented blossoms are also foraged for by people, and serve as markers to fruit gathering when spring and summer have been and gone.

Blackthorn trees are one of the most sought-out shrubs of liqueur-loving foragers in the autumn, who scramble hedgerows in the hunt for the astringent berries to add to alcohol to imbibe through the winter months. Across Europe, almost every nation has its own version of sloe liqueur, often using the drink of its national identity – for example, gin in Britain, grappa in Italy, schnapps in Germany and aquavit in Scandinavia. Some sloe drinks are simple affairs, made from a blend of berries, sugar and alcohol. Others, such as the Spanish *pacharán*, based on anise-flavoured liqueur, include additions such as coffee beans and spices. Whether you make sloe gin in Britain or *pacharán* in Spain, sloes have warmed the cockles through the winters for many years across many countries.

Appearing before the leaves, blackthorn blossom has white, five-petalled, edible flowers with yellow stamens. Gather to infuse in syrups and alcohol.

Young spring shoots, crimson-tinted before maturing into small, green, oval leaves. Tender new growth smells of almond when crushed and can be infused into liqueurs.

Black thorny twigs with leaf buds along the spine of the wood. Take care not to jab thorns into your skin.

Caution: Blackthorn spines can cause dramatic swelling from even the slightest graze – the black thorns contain high levels of alkaloids and phenolic compounds that result in major reactions, including swelling around the wound and sometimes nearby joints. Collect carefully.

Bluish-purple, 1–2cm-wide round fruits covered with a white yeast bloom that can be rubbed off to leave a shiny berry. Incredibly sour, the fruit sweeten the longer they are left on the shrub.

BLACKTHORN

Aside from liqueurs, the juice that is pressed or cooked out of sloes makes a sensational, lip-puckering, sour, liquid verjus, which can be used in place of vinegars in dressings or citrus in cocktails. Cooked with an equal ratio of sugar to juice, sloe juice transforms into a sensational, vitamin-C- and polyphenol-packed cordial.

Blackthorn blossom and young leaves can also be gathered, as one of the first plants to forage in the spring. Blossoms are delicate and delicious infused into sugar syrups with a squeeze of lemon – add when the syrup is hot and leave to infuse overnight. The leaves make an equally delicious, if less famous, drink than the berries.

BLACKTHORN LEAF LIQUEUR 'WINE OF THORNS'
Makes 1 litre

- A handful of freshly opened blackthorn leaf shoots, enough to loosely fill a 1-litre jar
- 100g sugar
- 750ml wine (colour of your choice)
- 200ml brandy

The leaves of blackthorn have an incredible almond perfume, and when infused in alcohol they make an ancient French aperitif known as *troussepinette*, or *épine*. This was originally made to be added to mediocre wines to improve them, and there are various recipes for it. Some use white wine, others rosé or red as a base; some fortify with brandy, others with vodka. This recipe is thought to be one of the originals, made in the Cognac region.

1. Add the freshly gathered leaves and tender stems to a wide-necked jar and cover with brandy then leave to macerate in a dark place for one month.

2. After a month, mix the sugar with the wine of your choice, and blend the brandy, leaves and sweetened wine together. Leave to mature for a further 2 months before filtering, bottling and drinking. Once open, keep in the fridge for up to a couple of months.

SPICED SLOE CHEESE
Makes 250g

- 250g ripe sloes
- 2 whole star anise
- Vanilla pod
- 250g sugar, warmed in the oven

Fruit cheeses are preserves that are thick enough to be cut into cubes but also have enough softness to be able to be spread. The tart fruitiness of sloes means they hold their own incredibly well in sugary preserves. If you want to swap some of the sloes for apples here, use the sourest you can find; ideally use wild crab apples and swap weight for weight.

1. Rinse the sloes and put them in a pan with 500ml of water along with the star anise and vanilla pod. Bring to a gentle simmer over a medium heat and cook for around 30 minutes until the sloes are very soft.

2. Tip the sugar into the pan and stir into the sloe mixture. When the sugar has dissolved, increase the heat and cook, stirring constantly, until very thick. Pass the pulp through a sieve. Spoon the thick mixture into oiled wide-necked jars or ramekins and seal with lids or cellophane discs.

You can turn the cheese into fruit pastilles by pouring the mixture into oiled ceramic baking trays and letting it set. When firm, chop into cubes and roll in sugar.

SLOE OLIVES
Makes a 200g jar

- 100g sloes
- 50g salt per 500ml mineral water

Just like olives, sloes have a large stone, are incredibly astringent when raw, and with the right treatment are great in a cocktail. Brining sloes in a salt solution produces a beautiful olive-like delicacy that can be plopped into a sloe gin martini.

1. Wash and rub the sloes dry (this is important, to remove the wild yeasts present in the white bloom on the skin), then pack into a bowl or pot. Combine one-part salt to ten-parts mineral (unchlorinated) water and pour over the sloes, ensuring they are well covered. Fill a clean freezer bag with water and push it into the top of the pot, to make sure the sloes are fully submerged, then set aside in a cool dark place for a week. (Check regularly to make sure the sloes are submerged.)

2. After a week fermenting in the briny solution, the sloes are ready to eat. They will keep in the fridge for up to a month, or if dehydrated and stored in an airtight container, up to a year. Use a slosh of the purple brine with sloe gin and vermouth to make Dirty Sloe Martinis (with the sloe olive to garnish.)

HOPS

Humulus lupulus

● **DISTRIBUTION**

Native to Europe and Asia, now naturalized in most countries.

● **HABITAT**

Hedgerows, along riverbanks and fen land.

● **GATHERING SEASONS**

Early–late spring:
Tender tips and leaves.

Late spring–late summer:
Older leaves.

Late summer–early autumn:
Hop flowers and fruit.

Thought to originate from China, hops have characteristic tough, clinging hairs that helped them twine across nations, establishing themselves across Asia and Europe. Thousands of years later, hops travelled oceans with beer-brewing farmers who established Australian and American hop farms; the bines no longer trailing hedgerows but forced skyward on tall poles, producing clusters of bitter green flowers in the late summer which end up in bittersweet beer that's drunk across the globe.

Hops and beer; you would be forgiven for assuming that hops have always been associated with the ancient art of brewing, but its addition to the alcoholic beverage is in fact a relatively modern affair. The first recorded use of hops in beer occurred in 822, at a monastery in northern France. Before then, herbs gathered from the wild such as yarrow and ground ivy were used in brewing, but hops' high level of antibacterial chemicals preserved beer for longer. Henceforth beer has been associated with the bitter, yeasty, fruity, almost garlicky flavour of hops. The tender shoots, leaves and flowers have, however, been eaten for far longer than they have been brewed. They have been gathered and consumed for thousands of years; the ancient Greeks, Egyptians and Romans ate hop shoots in green salads, as vegetables and medicine. High in vitamins E, C, B6 and phytoestrogens, which can mimic oestrogen, hops have a history of being used for boosting bone and heart health. The good news is that some of the beneficial elements of hops transfer into beer, but perhaps not enough to justify an extra pint!

Caution: Occasionally people can develop skin rashes after handling hops. Take note not to confuse hops with bryony, which is toxic; bryony has a smooth, glossy stem and spade-shaped shiny leaves.

Hop leaves are deeply lobed with toothed, rough edges. The leaves are mildly hoppy and can be infused as a flavouring.

Rust coloured square stem, becoming greener with age, bristly hairs on edges.

The hop shoots grow quickly after emerging from the ground each year. The tender tips are nutty and asparagus-like. You can also dig below the ground to harvest the blanched end of the shoots.

Green, cone-shaped flowers that turn into fruit only grow on female plants. The scaly fruit, used in brewing, contain lupinin, an aromatic bitter compound that gives beer its distinctive taste.

HOPS

The delicately flavoured, nutty shoots can be eaten raw in salads or, when they are slightly older (but still tender), quickly steamed and eaten as a vegetable with oil and lemon, added to warm salads or omelettes, or puréed into homemade pasta dough. Sixteenth-century Italian chef Bartolomeo Scappi recorded a recipe for battered fried hop shoots seasoned with orange juice, salt and pepper.

HOP, BORAGE, CHICORY AND BLOOD ORANGE SALAD
Serves 4

- 100g tender hop shoots
- 50g young borage leaves and flowers (or finely sliced cucumber)
- 100g chicory leaves (or young dandelion leaves and flowers)
- 50g toasted walnuts
- 1 blood orange, finely sliced

For the dressing:
- Zest and juice of 1 lemon
- Juice of 1 blood orange
- 30ml white balsamic vinegar
- 1 garlic clove, crushed
- ½ tsp salt
- ½ tsp black pepper
- 150ml extra virgin olive oil
- Honey to sweeten (optional)

Seventeenth-century recipes for hop shoot salads combine pepper, oranges, borage and bitter herbs –
all in season at the same time, in hedgerows and on market stalls. This salad is a welcome, vibrant treat with late winter colour and taste.

1. First make the dressing. Combine the citrus zest and juice, balsamic vinegar, garlic, salt and pepper in a bowl. Whisking the dressing, add the olive oil in a steady stream until combined. Transfer to a container and store in the fridge until needed.

2. Toss the hop shoots, borage, chicory leaves and walnuts in the dressing, and place in a serving dish with the blood orange slices.

3. Serve as a starter, or as a salad with oily fish or with a sharp cheese tart.

RISOTTO DI BRUSCANDOLI

Serves 4

- 1 tbsp extra virgin olive oil
- 200g hop shoots, rinsed and chopped into small pieces
- 1 knob of butter
- ½ medium onion, finely chopped
- 1 garlic clove, finely chopped
- 400g carnaroli or arborio rice
- 1 glass of white wine
- 1 litre chicken or vegetable stock
- 30g Parmesan cheese, finely grated
- Salt and freshly ground black pepper

Hops grow wild in the Veneto countryside, and every spring the vegetable markets around Venice's Rialto bridge sell bundles of hop shoots. Known in Italy as *bruscandoli,* the shoots are sold in the most part to turn into *risotto di bruscandoli* – Venetian hop shoot risotto.

1. Heat the oil in a pan and sauté the hop shoots for a few minutes until softened, then remove from the heat and set aside.

2. Melt the butter in a large frying pan, add the chopped onion and garlic and gently cook until the onion has softened. Add the rice and sauté for a minute until translucent. Pour in the wine and stir into the rice. Slowly start adding the stock, pouring in a little and adding more once it has been absorbed by the rice. Keep stirring the rice until it is cooked through. Hop shoot risotto is traditionally served quite sloppy, so add more stock if it looks too dry. Turn off the heat and vigorously stir in the grated Parmesan, season, and add the cooked hop shoots before serving.

HOP AND BRAMBLE WHISKY SOUR

Serves 4

- 100g blackberries (include red, unripe blackberries)
- 100ml sugar syrup
- 200ml juice from sour cooking or crab apples (extract by grating apples and squeezing out the juice)
- 300ml whisky
- Ice
- Hop flowers

Hop fruits ripen at the same time as blackberries and, if you are lucky, in the same hedgerows. Take an extra pot with you on your hop-foraging trips and you might be rewarded with two harvests. Whisky infused with blackberries alone is nice enough, but with the addition of hops, you have a wild delight.

1. Smash the blackberries using a pestle and mortar, add the sugar syrup and apple juice and pound the berries into a pulp. Push the sweetened pulp through a sieve into a cocktail shaker, add the whisky and shake.

2. Pour into a glass over ice and press a hop flower into the cocktail – the bitter flavours of the flower will start to infuse into the drink immediately. Serve with the hop flowers in the drink. The flowers can be taken out as soon as your drinker's perfect bitter levels have been met.

Sambucus nigra

Each leaf is made up of between five and seven feather-shaped leaflets, with serrated edges, growing in pairs opposite each other along the main leaf stem. Leaves are up to 30cm long and nearly as wide. Pungently scented, the leaves are not edible but are used externally to make soothing salves, traditionally applied to skin for bruising and sprains.

Elders grow as large shrubs or small trees. Older branches have a light grey-brown, deeply grooved bark; inside the wood is hollow and pithy; young elder branches are rough and green. The branches of elder are extremely easy to break, so take care when bending any branch to reach your harvest.

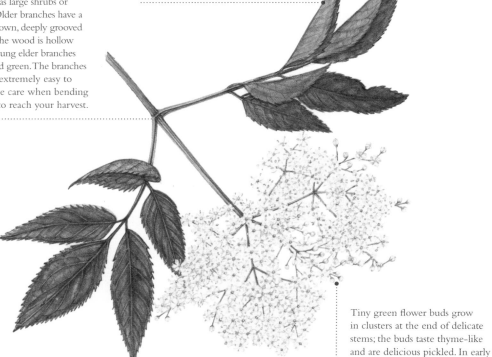

Tiny green flower buds grow in clusters at the end of delicate stems; the buds taste thyme-like and are delicious pickled. In early summer, the buds open into sprays of tiny pale cream flowers with yellow pollen, forming flat umbels 10–30cm across. Gather elderflowers when they are newly opened, before they lose their creamy pollen.

Caution: Take care not to confuse elder with toxic members of the carrot family – remember, elderflowers grow from a shrub. Berries, flowers and flower buds are the only edible parts of an elder. The berries need to be cooked or fermented before eating.

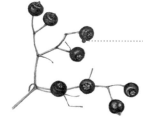

Initially dark green, elderberries turn russet red and finally almost black. The ripe berries are full of anthocyanin-rich purple-staining juice and small, hard seeds. Take care not to misidentify elderberries for inedible *Aralia Spinosa*, known as False or Prickly Elder due to its thorny bark.

ELDER

Sambucus spp.

❧ DISTRIBUTION

Widespread in temperate
and subtropical regions of
the world.

❧ HABITAT

Woodland, hedgerows,
gardens, scrubland and
wasteland; elder loves
potassium-rich soils
produced by wood ash
after fires.

**❧ GATHERING
SEASONS**

Mid–late spring:
Elderflower buds.

Early–midsummer:
Elderflowers.

Later summer–early autumn:
Ripe elderberries.

Throughout history, fairy tales, folklore and myths have been conjured up to keep children out of harm and adults in line, and not many trees have more tales of warning associated with them than the elder. In Scandinavian countries and in Britain, folk tales spoke of elder being a gateway into magical realms. Such a tree would need a special level of protection, and was guarded by Mother Elder who, whilst giving the trees' floral and berry-laden gifts to those who asked (politely), would curse death on those who broke off or burnt branches or destroyed the tree.

Whether the tree was a magical gateway or not, there was sense in the dark tale that although the flowers and berries are enchantingly delicious and almost magically medicinal, all other parts of the tree are poisonous.

Today, elder trees are flocked to in early summer; their cream sprays of the most fragrant flowers are plucked off the tree, destined to be infused into cordials, wines and champagnes. Lesser known, but equally delicious and valuable as a medicinal food, are the berries that droop from the laden branches in late summer and early autumn. The high-up flowers and purple-staining berries may tempt you to pull the limbs of the tree down so your harvest can be reached, but make sure you don't snap the boughs off the tree or Mother Elder might just get you!

ELDER

Elderflowers were traditionally gathered for their ability to help eliminate fevers, but today they are mostly used in sweet cordials and puddings. However, nibble on an elderflower and you will discover flavours of smoky herbs, which make it at home with savoury dishes. Stuff flowers into trout, stir them into lentil salads or dry the flowers and blend with sea salt and fennel seeds to create an indispensable seasoning.

ELDERBERRY AND LAVENDER JELLY
Makes 600g

- 1kg cooking apples or crab apples
- Juice of 1 lemon
- 1kg elderberries
- Sugar
- 3 sprigs of flowering lavender

This jelly is crammed full of an array of immune-boosting benefits and its flavour is equally sensational.

1. First, make the pectin (it helps flavour and set the jelly). Chop up the apples, place in a pan with the lemon juice, cover with water and cook over a medium heat, simmering until the apples are mushy. Transfer to a jelly bag or fine sieve and hang over a bowl overnight to collect the sticky pectin liquid that falls from the apple flesh.

2. To make the elderberry juice, gently heat the elderberries in a pan with a cup of water until they start to become soft and mushy. Using a masher, squash the juices out of the berries. Transfer the squashed berries and juice into a jelly bag and let the juice drip into a bowl. You can squeeze the bag with your hands to extract more juice but be aware that it stains.

3. Measure the total amount of apple pectin and elderberry juice; for every 150ml liquid, weigh out 100g sugar. Heat the pectin and half the elderberry juice in a wide pan, adding the sugar and lavender sprigs. Bring to a rolling boil until the jelly has reached its setting point – test this by dropping some of the hot liquid onto a cold plate and run a finger through the dollop; if it wrinkles, the jelly will set. At this point, take the pan off the heat, remove the lavender and add the remaining half of the elderberry juice to the hot mixture. Stir well and place back on the heat until the mixture reaches simmering point, then immediately pour into clean, sterilized jam jars and seal. Serve on toast to people with colds.

ELDERFLOWER FRITTERS
Serves 4

- Sunflower oil, for frying
- 1 large free-range organic egg
- 120ml ice-cold sparkling water
- 70g plain flour
- Pinch of fine salt
- 1½ tsp sugar
- 8 large heads of freshly picked elderflowers, shaken to remove insects
- Icing sugar, for dusting

Elderflower season can seem to go in the blink of an eye; a sudden rain deluge or heatwave can ruin hopes of a bumper harvest, but there are always a few latecomers to the elderflower party, and if you only have the chance to indulge in a few blooms, plunging them into hot oil, covered in batter, served with a sour frozen sherbet or ice cream is a treat that makes up for the lost crops.

1. Fill a large pan one-third full with sunflower oil and place over a medium heat.

2. Whilst the oil is heating, in a mixing bowl beat together the egg, half the water, the flour, salt and sugar and mix until lightly combined, then whisk in the rest of the water. Dip the flowers into the batter, shaking off any excess, place in the hot oil and fry for a few minutes until golden. Remove from the oil and place on a piece of kitchen roll to drain before dusting with icing sugar and serving immediately.

PICKLED ELDER BUDS IN GOOSEBERRY VINEGAR
Makes 300g

- 100g gooseberries
- 300ml apple cider vinegar
- 50g sugar
- 1 tsp salt
- 100g unopened elderflower buds, gathered just before they open while vibrant green and plump, washed and dried

Elderflower buds are intense and savoury in their flavour. Smoky, and reminiscent of thyme, they make incredible pickles when paired with summer fruit vinegars. Gooseberry and elderflowers are natural partners in sweet dishes and work just as well in this savoury pickle.

1. Place the gooseberries, vinegar, sugar and salt into a saucepan and slowly simmer until the gooseberries have collapsed. Take off the heat and leave to infuse overnight.

2. The next day, strain the vinegar into a pan (you can use the gooseberries in chutneys or with fish as a sauce) and reheat before pouring over the elderflower buds packed into a glass jar. Seal with lids suitable for vinegar and leave to mature for a few days before eating.

HONEYSUCKLE

Lonicera spp.

❧ **DISTRIBUTION**
Native to North America,
Europe and Asia, now
found globally apart from
in extremely dry or cold
climates.

❧ **HABITAT**
Gardens, hedgerows and
thickets. Thriving in rich soils
in full sun or partial shade.

❧ **GATHERING
SEASONS**
Early summer–mid autumn:
Flowers.

Dusk in summer months is sweetened by the perfume of nectar–rich honeysuckle. Its flowers linger through the summer, often well into autumn, giving people plenty of time to gather the sweet blooms – long-seasoned, beautiful, scented flowers that everybody recognizes. Children grow up sucking the nectar from honeysuckles; surely they must be one of the easiest plants to gather from? Maybe, but not quite.

Nature is a generous giver but it likes to make us work just a bit for our sweet rewards, and honeysuckle needs a bit more of your attention than you might first think, because honeysuckle isn't simply honeysuckle – there are over 180 varieties adorning the globe, many growing in lands far away from their native locations. Moved and altered by plant breeders, they often escape into the wild and whilst many of the varieties of honeysuckle flowers you find may indeed be edible, some are not, and a few are very toxic.

The caution that comes with eating honeysuckle is an important one to remember for any edible wild plant that has gone from wild to cultivated. Plants whose parentage includes edible qualities may lose their 'safe to consume' label through breeding just as they gain other, more horticultural, features. The safest way to ensure you correctly identify any plant you might want to graze from is to note the plant's key botanical features and use its unique, globally used Latin name to identify it. Start with learning to identify the illustrated common honeysuckle (*Lonicera periclymenum*) and Japanese honeysuckle (*Lonicera japonica*), which has smaller, creamier flowers and black berries (which are inedible like the red berries of the common honeysuckle). Both of these are fortunately amongst the most common honeysuckles and also fortunately happen to both produce edible flowers. Once you can identify them and discover their incredible perfumed flavour, you will soon discover why a bit of botanical homework is well worth the effort.

Lonicera periclymenum

Long tubular petals split open, curling back as they age to reveal long stamens, which join together at the base with green nodules, forming a bobbled centre. Common honeysuckle has petals that appear vivid pink before they open, folding back to reveal a pale pink or white colouring. Japanese honeysuckle has smaller, pale yellow-white flowers.

Caution: The tale of eating honeysuckle is a delicious one, but not all species are edible, so take care in your identification.

Oval leaves have smooth edges, growing in pairs opposite each other.

Honeysuckle berries are often red, blue or black. Most species of honeysuckle have inedible berries; whilst toxic to people they are important food sources for birds including thrushes and bullfinches.

HONEYSUCKLE

Honeysuckles are beautiful in cooling recipes during the warm summer months. Remove the bitter green balls at the base of the flowers before infusing in long drinks, vinegar, ice creams and poaching liquid for chicken and fish. Honeysuckle flowers make stunning liqueurs – a couple of hours soaking in vodka releases their flavour, which can then be paired with sodas or fruit juices. Honeysuckle flowers not only taste beautiful, but they are also rich in antimicrobial and anti-inflammatory properties, and they are one of the most widely used herbs in Chinese medicine. Honeysuckle flowers dry extremely well and can be used throughout the winter in teas and throat-soothing syrups.

HONEYSUCKLE AND TARRAGON SORBET
Serves 4

- 750ml water, just boiled
- 1-litre bowl of honeysuckle flowers, gathered in the evening
- 1 sprig of tarragon
- 100g sugar
- Juice of 2 lemons

Japanese honeysuckle grows abundantly and invasively in southern areas of the United States, where its scent fills the hot summer nights. Honeysuckle sorbet is a favourite cooler for just those sweetly scented, sticky evenings.

1. Pour the just-boiled water over the honeysuckle flowers and tarragon in a heatproof bowl, then stir in the sugar and leave to infuse for 30 minutes.

2. Squeeze in the lemon juice (if you are lucky, the honeysuckle-infused liquid will turn pink), then strain and pour the liquid into an ice-cream maker and churn until the sorbet is frozen. Serve immediately – the low sugar levels in the sorbet means that it will freeze solid if put in the freezer. If you do freeze it – for example, if you do not have an ice-cream maker – turn it into a granita by scraping the flavoured ice apart with a fork.

HONEYSUCKLE CORDIAL

Makes 2 litres

....

- 1kg sugar
- 1-litre container of honeysuckle flowers
- 1 tsp citric acid
- Juice of 1 lemon

....

Honeysuckle cordial makes a beautiful soft drink, or a grown-up addition to cocktails such as juleps and margaritas. Drizzle the cordial over warm cakes, fruit salads and pancakes, or stir into apple cider or rice wine vinegar to make floral salad dressings.

1. Boil 1 litre of water and the sugar in a large pan until the sugar has dissolved, then leave to cool for 10 minutes, before pouring over the flowers. Stir in the citric acid and lemon, cover, cool and allow to steep in the fridge for 24 hours.

2. Warm again before straining through a double layer of muslin. Bottle and pasteurize (see page 9) or keep in the fridge and use within a few weeks.

STEAMED FISH WITH HONEYSUCKLE

Serves 4

....

- 750g mild white fish fillets (such as snapper)
- 4 tbsp Chinese rice wine
- 3 tbsp sesame oil
- 2 or 3 slices of fresh root ginger
- 1 tbsp light soy sauce
- 50g honeysuckle flowers
- Salt and freshly ground black pepper

....

This Chinese recipe balances the gently perfumed flavour of honeysuckle with ginger and salty soy and is delicious served with jasmine rice or noodles with pickled vegetables.

1. Run your fingers lightly over the fish to make sre there are no bones. Mix together the Chinese rice wine, sesame oil, ginger slices and light soy sauce and season with salt and pepper, rub onto the fish and leave for 30 minutes to marinate.

2. Place the fish, marinade liquid and honeysuckle flowers on a large piece of baking paper lined with tin foil, seal the paper and foil around the fish and cook in a steamer or in the oven, preheated to 190°C, 375°F, gas mark 5, for 15–20 minutes or until the fish flakes easily.

Rosa champlain

Hips: Rosa rugosa, Rosa cannina, Rosa pimpinellifolia

Roses produce nectar from the base of the flower, a part known as the hypanthium, which also provides the base for the petals, stamens and sepals. No matter how many petals the rose has, all roses have rounded, symmetrical flower heads, with evenly distributed petals. The texture of all rose petals is silky and cool to the touch and they have traditionally been associated with cooling in Ayurveda and other medicines.

The rose family is vast, but nearly every species (bar a few evergreen roses) within it have sets of oval-shaped, serrated leaflets growing in alternate patterns along a main leaf stem.

Most roses are pollinated by insects and produce fruit in a structure known as a hip. Hips can vary widely in colour, shape and flavour. The flesh of all rose hips is edible, but needs processing to avoid ingesting the seeds and hairs.

ROSE

Rosa spp.

DISTRIBUTION

Global, native to Europe,
northwest Africa, west Asia.
Introduced to America,
New Zealand.

HABITAT

Hedgerows and gardens,
sandy coastal areas, open
clearings in woodland.

**GATHERING
SEASONS**

Late spring–early autumn:
Rose petals.

Late summer–early winter:
Rose hips.

Roses twist through hedgerows, adorn gardens, walls, parks and shorelines, urban and rural landscapes. Cherished like few other plants, roses have wound themselves into the hearts of most nations across the world, from India to the Middle East, western Europe to Mexico; wherever roses bloom their beauty makes us fall in love with them.

Fossils of this distinctive plant have been found scattered across continents – some dating back 40 million years; wherever early nomadic people travelled to, roses appear to scatter petals in their path. Our long love affair with roses in food is documented over millennia; 5,000-year-old clay tablets from Mesopotamia document the leader of the world's first empire taking roses on his military campaigns to plant in the countries he conquered, including modern-day Turkey. Texts of 4,000 years ago found in tombs refer to making vast amounts of rose water to fill thousands of jars which were used each year to scent sultans' palaces and feasts. Other texts dating back 3,000 years describe roses being pounded into sugars and made into delicious medicinal pills. By the time of the Roman Empire, huge rose gardens were cultivated, supplying the Empire's insatiable demand for perfumed rose oil to flavour food, and scent rooms and people.

Our culinary infatuation with the perfumed blooms has wilted recently, since roses became regarded as ornamentals to be seen but not eaten. Rose flavouring is now sought from specialist shops rather than the plants nearby. Like the fossils that were excavated across continents, roses now adorn most gardens throughout the world, their delicious flavours waiting patiently to be unearthed and discovered once again.

ROSE

Whether wild or cultivated, all rose species are edible; their flavour varies like the scent – some are fruity, others perfumed, others bordering on bitter. Roses all produce vitamin-C-laden hips, ranging from dark brown chocolate-flavoured to bright red hips that taste of apples, oranges and tomatoes. Take care not to consume the fine hairs and seeds inside the fruit as they act as an irritant. If you use thick-fleshed hips, you can scoop out the hairs and seeds; otherwise, cook the hips or juice them with water to release their goodness then strain through a very fine muslin cloth.

ROSE HIP, SUMAC AND CHILLI JAM
Makes 600g

- 1kg cooking apples or crab apples
- 150g rose hips
- 1 tsp sumac powder
- Cider vinegar
- Granulated sugar
- 1 red chilli, cut into the finest slivers possible

The fruity vibrancy of rose hips is beautiful preserved as a sweet jelly or syrup, but paired with savoury ingredients the tomato flavours within the hips come alive.

1. Peel and core the apples, placing peel and cores in a pan with the rose hips and sumac. Cover with water and cook for around 20 minutes, until the hips are soft. Purée the mixture and strain through a muslin cloth, then measure the strained juice and for every 100ml add 10ml of cider vinegar.

2. Heat the vinegar and apple and rose hip mixture in a pan and add two-thirds of the volume of sugar to the liquid, bring to the boil and keep the mixture at a rolling boil until it has reached the point of setting. (Test for setting point using a sugar thermometer – it should reach 105°C – or by dropping a teaspoon of liquid onto a cold plate – the liquid will set and should wrinkle when you push it with your finger.)

3. Let the mixture cool slightly and stir in slivers of chilli according to your taste. Pour into sterilized jars to store the jelly for up to a year.

ROSE PETAL RICE PUDDING

Serves 4

- Petals from 3 large roses, the bitter white ends snipped off
- 40g sugar
- 150g short grain rice
- 500ml full-fat milk (or coconut milk)
- A few cardamom seeds
- 150ml whipped cream (or coconut cream)
- Chopped pistachios

Roses have a long history within Indian and Ayurvedic food, regarded as a sweet but at the same time bitter, hydrating, oily and cooling herb. Kheers are cool rice puddings that have been made in India for over 2,000 years. (In southern India, the dairy milk is often replaced with coconut milk.)

1. Place the roses in a mortar and cover with 1 teaspoon of water and the sugar. Pound until the roses start breaking down into the sugar and set aside.

2. Place the rice and milk with the cardamom in a pan and cook over a low heat for about 25 minutes, continually stirring until the rice is soft. Add the rose petals and sugar, cooking for a few minutes, then set aside to cool.

3. As soon as the rice is cool, fold in the cream and spoon into individual bowls. Place in the fridge to chill before serving with chopped pistachios.

ROSE PETALS MACERATED IN SUGAR

Makes 300g

- 200g sugar
- 100g fresh rose petals

Macerating roses for weeks in sugar makes an intensely flavoured paste, known as gulkand, it was used for flavouring and for its cooling medicinal properties. This practice is almost as old as the records are for roses, used in Persia and India to preserve the perfume of the petals.

1. In a jar, sprinkle a layer of sugar, followed by a layer of rose petals, layering until the last roses are covered. Cover the rose and sugar layers with a disc of baking paper and a tight-fitting lid and place either in the sun or in a cool dark place for a month. Sun-baked rose sugar takes on a slightly caramelized flavour like gulkand. After a month the sugar and roses can be blended into a paste or the rose petals removed and eaten and the sticky sugary paste used as a heavenly flavouring.

WILD BLUEBERRY

Vaccinium spp.

❧ DISTRIBUTION

Northern Europe, Iceland,
Asia, North America,
introduced to cooler areas
of Australia.

❧ HABITAT

Acidic heathlands, moors and
forest clearings, mainly in
hilly areas.

**❧ GATHERING
SEASONS**

Spring–autumn:
Leaves.

Summer–early autumn:
Fruits.

Wild blueberries are low-growing perennial shrubs that thrive in coniferous forests and hills across the northern half of the globe. Take a walk onto acidic heathland during summer months and you'll often find yourself walking alongside wild blueberry shrubs that grow amongst swathes of purple heather flowers.

As beautiful as these habitats are to walk in, the acid soils and exposed places in which wild blueberries flourish make them hard landscapes for people to live in. Even thousands of years ago, when most people favoured lower valleys to dwell in, journeys to seek out the little fruit involved long walks up hills and mountainsides. When the crops were finally found, it took hours of work to gather enough of the tiny berries to fill a basket. And yet, people looked forward to the wild blueberry harvest with such relish that in many areas gathering the first of the purple fruits became a symbolic harvest, and a longed-for one at that. In the years before fresh food imports, wild blueberries were amongst the first fruit available after the previous year's stores had run out. The intensely fruity berries are crammed full of vitamin C, pro-vitamin A, minerals and health-giving fruit acids, and their ripening would have been a day worth celebrating. And so it was. In Ireland a harvest festival celebrated on Fraughan Sunday was named after the berries, when throngs of young people would climb the hills and gather basketfuls of the newly ripened fruit. Even without the lure of a Celtic festival, northern European families would eagerly await the day on which the wild blueberries that covered one-fifth of the land would ripen. The insanely delicious taste of the first berries of the year made the longest of hikes worthwhile.

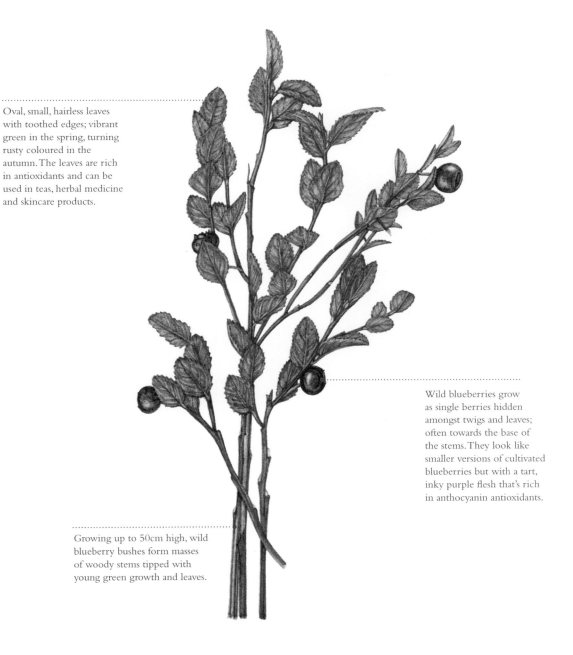

Oval, small, hairless leaves with toothed edges; vibrant green in the spring, turning rusty coloured in the autumn. The leaves are rich in antioxidants and can be used in teas, herbal medicine and skincare products.

Wild blueberries grow as single berries hidden amongst twigs and leaves; often towards the base of the stems. They look like smaller versions of cultivated blueberries but with a tart, inky purple flesh that's rich in anthocyanin antioxidants.

Growing up to 50cm high, wild blueberry bushes form masses of woody stems tipped with young green growth and leaves.

Vaccinium myrtillus

WILD BLUEBERRY

Wild blueberries used to be both gorged on fresh and dried for later in the year. Preserved by being spread out on trays and dried in the sun, the resulting wild blueberry currants can be added to soups and stews and ground into fruity seasonings with salt and pepper. The dried fruit is delicious sprinkled over breakfast porridge, or used in baking – adding anthocyanin-rich flecks to soda breads and Christmas cakes.

WILD BLUEBERRY AND BAY PASTRIES
Serves 6

- 1 sheet (320g) ready rolled puff pastry
- 350ml full-fat milk
- 3 fresh bay leaves
- 2 egg yolks
- 20g flour
- 20g cornflour
- 25g sugar
- 100g wild blueberries
- Icing sugar, for dusting

Many countries have recipes for wild blueberries in pies – inky berries and pastry are almost impossible to improve on, but a good custard makes even the best pies better.

1. Preheat the oven to 200°C, 400°F, gas mark 6.

2. Roll out a sheet of puff pastry on a sheet of greaseproof paper and lift both onto a baking tray. Score the pastry to make 6 × 10cm rectangles and cook until golden and puffed up.

3. Meanwhile, make the bay-infused crème pâtissière by gently heating the milk, then add the bay leaves, remove from the heat and leave to infuse for 15 minutes.

4. Mix the egg yolks in a bowl with the flour, cornflour, sugar and 50ml of the warm milk until smooth, then blend into the remaining bay-infused milk. Return the mixture to the pan and stir over the heat until it has thickened. If you wish, you can whip the leftover egg whites and then gently stir them into the crème pâtissière, off the heat. Leave the crème to cool.

5. Break the pastry into rectangles along the scorings, then slice in between the layers to create tops and bottoms. Dollop a spoonful of crème pâtissière on the bottom layer, and sprinkle with wild blueberries. Top with the other half of the pastry and dust with icing sugar.

WILD BLUEBERRY SOUP – BLÅBÄRSSOPPA

Serves 4

- 350g wild blueberries, fresh or defrosted
- 50g sugar
- 700ml water
- 1½ tbsp potato flour or cornflour

Wild blueberry soup is made in Sweden and Finland and is famously served at the world's oldest and longest ski marathon, when skiers drink hot blåbärssoppa to sustain them during the race.

1. Place the berries and a splash of water in a pan, and gently cook until the berries start to collapse. Add the rest of the water and sugar and bring to a gentle simmer for 10–15 minutes.

2. Meanwhile, in a small bowl, blend the potato flour to a smooth paste with a little water.

3. Take the cooked berries off the heat and slowly stir in the potato flour paste. Place the pan back onto a low heat, stirring until the mixture starts thickening.

4. Serve hot, on a ski slope, or cold under the midnight sun.

WILD BLUEBERRY PIEROGIS

Makes 20

- 500g plain flour, plus extra for dusting
- Pinch of salt
- 1 egg, beaten
- Oil, for greasing
- 100g wild blueberries
- Icing sugar or salted butter, to serve (optional)

Across many Slavic countries wild blueberries are stuffed into dumplings. Pierogis are Poland's version of dumplings, and these can be frozen to eat after the berries have disappeared from the hillsides.

1. Put the flour and salt in a mixing bowl and gradually stir in the egg and enough warm water to bring it together to form a dough. Tip out the dough and knead lightly for 2–3 minutes, then rub a little oil all over it before covering with a damp tea towel. Leave to rest for 30 minutes.

2. Flour a work surface and roll out 20 circles of dough, around 3mm thick. Place a spoonful of wild blueberries on half of the circle, dampen all round the edge with water then fold the other half over the filling and press together to seal the berries in the dough. Cover the pierogis with a damp cloth while you make the rest.

3. Bring a large pan of water to the boil, then drop in the pierogis, a few at a time, and cook for about 3 minutes, or until they rise to the top of the pan. Drain and serve immediately, scattering icing sugar over the dumplings to sweeten them, or fry them in salted butter before serving.

First-year blackberry stems are ridged with
soft young thorns. As the year progresses,
the stems become very long, bending over
and resting on the ground where they root,
eventually forming thickets associated with
brambles in overgrown areas. The young
shoots and soft-forming thorns are edible,
with a sour, salty flavour.

Blackberry leaves grow in early spring; pale
downy buds develop into new sets of leaves,
which grow alternately along the main stem.
Each leaf is divided into three or five serrated
and pointed oval leaflets. Leaf buds are
astringent with a coconut flavour; the leaves
are tannic and used to make medicinal teas.

Small, pale pink or white flowers develop
into clusters of fruit; small green berries grow
and ripen through the summer, changing
from green to red and finally an inky bluish-
black. The fruit at the tip of a cluster tends to
be the sweetest, making gathering as soon as
the fruits start ripening worthwhile.

BLACKBERRY

Rubus fruticosus

🌿 DISTRIBUTION

Globally, apart from
in Antarctica.

🌿 HABITAT

Wasteland, hedgerows,
clearings in both rural
and urban areas.

**🌿 GATHERING
SEASONS**

Spring:
Leaf buds and tender
young stems.

Summer:
Leaves and flowers.

Early autumn:
Fruit.

If anyone, child or adult, rural or city dweller, stands by a blackberry thicket dripping with ripe fruit they will feel an almost instinctive urge to gather. Almost without thinking, their hands will plunge into the bush, navigating without fear the brutal thorns to pluck the fruit that we are almost born knowing we can eat. In that very moment they become a gatherer, doing the same thing that people have ever since they first ate the fruit; they could be anywhere in time, anywhere in the world.

Whilst many wild plants that we used to eat have been forgotten, there is something about blackberries that has kept a fragment of people's hunter-gatherer instinct alive. Perhaps it's the berries' sweet perfumed taste. Although they can often be sour, or even bitter, maybe it's the regularity of the berry that makes it safe? Though there are hundreds of hybrids of blackberry, all with different characteristics, bramble has remained the plant we feel safe gathering, when all else around it has become alien. Blackberries were gorged on because they were good (even with their sweet, sour, bitter flavour roulette), but from Greece to America, people also chewed on leaves to treat ulcers and diarrhoea – which has been proven by modern science to be exactly the right thing to do.

Our modern lives are a million miles from those lived by our ancestors; within a short space of time we have been removed from our natural habitats, disconnected from the natural world, forgetting that we are part of it as well. But the fact that stumbling upon a thicket of black fruits triggers within us an urge to reach out and pop the berry into our mouths is a welcome reminder that the gatherer is still within us, waiting to fill baskets once more.

BLACKBERRY

Blackberries are probably the most widely eaten wild fruit. Gobbling the berries by the handful in the warm autumn sun is hard to beat. Gather a mixture of sweet and sour berries and your hands might be prickled but your cupboard will be full of delicious flavours for the winter. As soon as you pick your berries, keep them cool – if you have not got time to process them immediately, freeze them until you do.

BLACKBERRY BUD PANNA COTTA
Serves 4

- 3 gelatine leaves, or equivalent amount of agar agar
- 400ml full-fat milk
- 100ml double cream
- A handful of freshly picked blackberry buds
- 10g sugar
- Gorse flowers (optional)

Infusing the young leaf buds into syrups or milks releases their coconut sweetness, allowing desserts such as panna cotta to be made with the minimal amount of added sugar. Blackberries often twist through gorse bushes and their buds form as gorse flowers bloom. The flowers and buds are a flavour pairing made in spiky heaven. (Oat milk is an ideal alternative to dairy in this recipe.)

1. Soak the gelatine leaves in a little bowl of cold water for 5–10 minutes, until soft.

2. Meanwhile, place the milk, cream, buds and sugar into a pan and heat until warm. Take off the heat and leave to infuse for 1 hour.

3. After this time, using clean hands, rub and squeeze the softened buds in the liquid – they will release a pale green colour into the milk. Strain the milk through a fine sieve, pour it back into the pan and reheat. Remove from the heat, and add the gelatine leaves, squeezing out any water from them first, and stir until the gelatine has dissolved.

4. Divide the mixture among four ramekins, then leave to cool before placing them in the fridge for at least an hour, until set.

5. Serve decorated with gorse flowers, if you like.

PICKLED UNRIPE BLACKBERRIES

Makes 500g

- Enough unripe blackberries to fill a 500g jar
- 300ml apple cider vinegar
- 100g sugar
- ½ tsp coriander seeds
- 1 tbsp chopped-up pine needles
- ½ tsp fennel seeds
- ½ tsp salt
- ½ cinnamon stick

Maroon-hued, fully formed but not yet ripened blackberries are crunchy, sour, fruity and full of delicious potential.

1. Pull off any remaining stems from the blackberries and place the fruit in a bowl of cold water, gently rubbing the berries with your hands in the water to release any debris and spiny hairs. Tip the berries into a colander, rinse under running water, then leave to drain.

2. Add all the other ingredients to a stainless-steel pan set over a medium heat, then bring to a simmer and keep on the heat until the liquid has reduced by about one-third. Take off the heat and leave to infuse for half an hour before straining out the flavourings through a fine-mesh sieve.

3. Pack the blackberries into a sterilized jar, reheat the strained pickling vinegar in a small pan and pour it over the berries while hot, so that there is enough liquid to completely cover them. Leave the jars for a few minutes before sealing, as you may need to top up with more liquid once the berries have settled.

4. Seal the jars, and store at room temperature for up to 6 months.

BLACKBERRY, LEMON AND APPLE OAT CRUMBLE

Serves 4

- 150g rolled oats
- 100g golden caster sugar
- Zest and juice of 1 organic lemon
- 100g salted butter, frozen
- 2 large apples
- 500g blackberries
- Custard, to serve

The British have such affection for this fruit pudding, you would be forgiven for thinking it had been made for centuries, but in fact crumbles were only created during rationing in World War II. Necessity is sometimes the mother of delicious invention.

1. Place 100g of the oats into a food processor and blend to a flour, then tip into a mixing bowl and stir in the sugar, lemon zest and remaining oats. Grate the butter into the oat mixture and, using your fingers, rub together to form crumbs.

2. Preheat the oven to 175°C, 325°F, gas mark 3. Peel, core and chop the apples into cubes and put in a baking dish, then toss them in the lemon juice and stir in the blackberries. Cover with the oaty crumb mixture, forking the top of the crumble to create a fluffy texture.

3. Cook for 25–30 minutes or until golden. Remove and leave to cool slightly before serving with custard.

SEA BUCKTHORN

Hippophae rhamnoides

❧ DISTRIBUTION

Originating in the Himalayas,
sea buckthorn is now
naturalized across Asia,
Europe and Canada.

❧ HABITAT

Needing full sun and well-
drained ground to thrive, sea
buckthorn can be found on
sand dunes, cliffs, hillsides
and planted in gardens as an
ornamental hedging plant.

❧ GATHERING SEASONS

Spring–autumn:
Leaves for tea.

Late summer–late winter:
Berries – these will shrivel
slightly as they age on
the plant.

Bright orange sea buckthorn berries adorn silvery leaved spiny shrubs that form thickets on coastlines across Europe and North America. They may appear native to the shoreline, but sea buckthorn's homeland is very different. Originating high in the Himalayan mountains, sea buckthorn grows into gnarly-limbed trees, forming groves of cherished woodland protected by local monks. Rich in active ingredients including antioxidants and flavonoids, the berries contain vast amounts of vitamins C, E and B-complex, with 7 per cent of the berry being made up from fats, which, unlike any other plant food, contains all four omega oils. Sea buckthorn is known in its homeland as the Holy Fruit and has been used for thousands of years in Chinese, Indian and Tibetan medicines.

Legends tell of Mongolian horse herders who would take weary, ill animals to graze on sea buckthorn, the omega oils restoring their health and the gloss in their coats. The connection between sea buckthorn and equine health also contributed to the relentless expansion of the Greek Empire during the rule of Alexander the Great; as his exhausted troops rode through sea buckthorn-filled landscapes, the weakened horses started eating berries from the tree, and when they almost miraculously regained energy and their coats shone, the equally fatigued soldiers did the same. Like the horses, they regained their strength, leading to sea buckthorn becoming a secret weapon in the hands of empire-growing warriors right until the ultimate warlord, Genghis Khan, who put his own vast empire down to the power he gained from the bright orange, fat-laden berry.

Silvery grey, long narrow leaves, reminiscent of olive leaves, sea buckthorn leaves are rich in antioxidant polyphenols and can be used as a tea or in skincare preparations.

Rounded, bright orange fruit no bigger than 1cm in diameter cover the branches. The thin skin of the fruit bursts easily, revealing very juicy, incredibly sour, edible pulp and small dark seeds.

Thorny branches, growing as a shrub or from a main trunk as a small tree.

Caution: If you are on a blood-thinning or blood sugar-lowering medication, seek advice before using sea buckthorn.

SEA BUCKTHORN

For all of its strengths, sea buckthorn provides challenges to anyone wanting to eat it; firstly, the vitamin-C-packed berries grow amongst spear-like defences that need military precision to navigate between; once you capture your prize, unless you handle them with care the berries can squash, exploding their orange juices before you have the chance to eat them. Many people cut off the end branches, laden with berries, to freeze and pluck off stems as they need them. Alternatively, you can wait until a cold night's frost has semi-solidified the fruit then shake or strip the berries from the spiny plant.

SEA BUCKTHORN VINEGAR
Makes 300ml

- 125g sea buckthorn berries
- 300ml white wine vinegar or cider vinegar
- 125g sugar

This vinegar is a pale-coloured but fruity flavoured Scandinavian delicacy which is delicious added to sparkling water or used in salad dressings and sauces. Adding the sugar once the berries have been removed from the vinegar allows you to control the sweetness. Some recipes add a sprig of rosemary to the bottle, which gives an additional herbal flavour.

1. Thoroughly rinse the berries, discarding any that are damaged.

Place them in a sterilized, wide-mouthed jar suitable for vinegars (such as a Kilner jar), cover with 250ml of the vinegar, seal and place on a sunny windowsill for 4 weeks.

2. After 4 weeks, gently pour the berries into a sieve lined with doubled-up muslin cloth or a coffee filter set over a bowl to strain the liquid of any impurities.

3. Whilst you are straining the berries, dissolve 125g sugar in 50ml hot water and the remaining 50ml vinegar. Let the sweetened liquid cool and add small amounts to the sea buckthorn-infused vinegar, tasting until it reaches your preferred level of sweetness. Pour into sterilized bottles with vinegar-proof lids. Fruit vinegars keep indefinitely but are at their best used within a year.

SEA BUCKTHORN CURD

Makes 250g

- 100ml sea buckthorn juice
- 100g sugar
- 50g salted butter, cubed
- 3 egg yolks and 1 whole egg

The acidic flavours of sea buckthorn berries are perfectly paired with the richness of butter in a fruit curd. Serve on buttered bread, rippled through ice cream, or dolloped onto pillowy meringues alongside slices of mango to create a pudding bursting with the most vibrant of flavours.

1. Put the sea buckthorn juice, sugar and butter in a heatproof bowl over a pan of simmering water. Gently heat the mixture, stirring until the butter has melted.

2. In a separate bowl, beat the egg and yolks. Stir into the sea buckthorn mixture, keeping it on the heat and continually stirring for about 10 minutes, until the curd has become thick.

3. Remove from the heat and stir occasionally as the curd cools. Pour into sterilized jars and seal. This will keep for a couple of weeks in the fridge.

EXTRACTING SEA BUCKTHORN JUICE

Once you have gathered your berries, you can simply plunge them into honey or vinegar or dehydrate them to store for later use. However, most recipes call for juice rather than whole berries, and mastering the art of turning the berries into orange liquid is worth doing to make sea buckthorn curd alone.

1. Pull the berries from the stalks, in the direction of the leaves, dropping the berries and their juice into a bowl. Mash the fruit and juices with your hands or a potato masher and press the pulp through a sieve, squeezing out as much of the pulp as possible. The liquid at this point is rich in vitamin C, and can be preserved by freezing in ice-cube trays until needed, to keep the optimal amount of vitamin C, or cooked into curds or syrups.

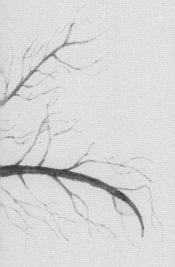

PERENNIALS

Perennial plants grow for longer than two years, often dying back in the winter to produce new shoots and growth in the following year. Many edible perennials emerge in the spring, offering a rolling crop of roots, shoots, buds, flowers and seeds before they disappear under the ground until the following year. The long-lived nature of perennials is a bonus to foragers, who can return to the same spot each year to gather from the plant as it grows through the seasons.

THREE-CORNERED LEEK

Allium triquetrum

◕ DISTRIBUTION

Native to the Mediterranean
area, naturalized across
Europe, Britain, America,
Australia and New Zealand.

◕ HABITAT

Meadows, clearings,
hedgerows, roadsides
and gardens.

**◕ GATHERING
SEASONS**

Late autumn–early spring:
Younger grassy stems.

Late spring–early summer:
Longer flowering stems and
flowers, bulbs and seed pods.

Three-cornered leeks are wild onions, with snowdrop-like flowers and a tender, mild flavour that sits between garlic and onion. This elegant plant is a traditional part of the cuisine of many Mediterranean islands. The three-cornered leek was spread across the world during the eighteenth century, moved out of its native regions by plant collectors, who introduced it to areas such as the southwest of Britain where it was cultivated as a pungent, yet ornamental plant. Once out of their native environments, in cooler climates where it was easier to grow, the plant established itself with vigour and, with the aid of an unexpected helper, was swiftly transported out of the confines of flower beds. The assistant in its spread was the humble ant – three-cornered leeks belong to a group of plants that produce bulbs coated with a nutritious food for ant larvae. Ants carry newly formed bulbs to their nests, where the young gorge on the outer layer of the bulb, leaving the less-palatable inner part to germinate and start growing a new clump, appearing randomly some distance from the original colony. Three-cornered leeks are rampant in their clever onward push, growing in lush swathes across landscapes. Though delicious, it is regarded as a highly invasive plant, and you will not be frowned upon for uprooting this interloper, which is fortunate because all parts of the plant, including the bulbs, are delicious. Ants, it turns out, have good taste.

Long, fleshy, grass-like blades, with a pronounced 'V' shape and distinct onion smell. Mild onion taste, ideal chopped into salads, soups or sauces.

Six-petalled white flower with a green stripe down the centre. An onion-flavoured addition to salads. Seedheads the size of garden peas with black seeds inside, that can be eaten raw or pickled.

Small white bulbs and bulbils can be cooked, pickled and fermented. The tendrilled roots have a buttery onion flavour and are excellent deep-fried and salted.

Triangular profile. Mild and crunchy. Delicious wilted in white wine, oil or butter. Serve as you would leeks.

Caution: Snowdrops and white bluebells, both of which are inedible, look very similar to the three-cornered leek – learn to identify these plants before gathering the three-cornered leek. Observe the leaf structure and the flower, with its lime-green line, to ensure you've selected the right plant.

THREE-CORNERED LEEK

Easily interchanged with recipes calling for leeks, onions or garlic, three-cornered leek is used in salads, sauces, risottos, pestos, soups and tarts. Chop into potato salads or infuse into vinegars. Three-cornered leeks preserve well with fermentation; the stalks, flower heads and bulbs lend themselves to pickling, especially with fennel- or thyme-infused vinegars.

THREE-CORNERED LEEK HOMITY PIE
Serves 4

- 300g shortcrust pastry
- Flour, for dusting
- 450g three-cornered leek
- 3 tbsp oil
- 25g butter
- 350g potatoes, peeled and chopped into 2cm cubes
- 100g cheddar cheese, grated
- 1 tbsp milk, plus extra for brushing
- 15g parsley, chopped
- Sea salt and freshly ground black pepper

Three-cornered leeks replace onions in this wild version of a classic British savoury pie, which was eaten during rationing around World War II.

1. Roll out half the pastry on a lightly dusted work surface, then use it to line a 20cm pie dish and place in the fridge to chill. Wrap the remaining pastry in cling film and place in the fridge.

2. Preheat the oven to 220°C, 425°F, gas mark 7.

3. Chop the three-cornered leek into 5cm lengths, sauté in a saucepan with some oil and butter until soft, then add the chopped potatoes, put the lid on and sweat for 5 minutes. Remove from the heat and stir in half the cheese and the milk and season with salt and pepper. Leave the mixture to cool.

4. While the mixture cools, roll out the reserved pastry on a lightly floured work surface to make a lid for the pie.

5. Stir the parsley into the cooled mixture, then fill the pie case with it, scattering the remaining cheese on top, and pop the pastry lid on top. Seal the lid around the rim, then brush the pastry with a little milk and sprinkle over a pinch of sea salt.

6. Bake in the oven for 25 minutes or until golden.

BALSAMIC-ROASTED THREE-CORNERED LEEK BULBS

Makes 100g

- 1 tbsp balsamic vinegar
- 1 tbsp olive oil
- 1 tsp chopped fresh thyme
- 1 tsp chopped fresh oregano
- 1 tsp sugar
- Pinch of salt
- Approx. 100g three-cornered leek bulbs, popped out of the outer layer of the base of the plant

The bulbs of three-cornered leeks are at the base of the plant, just above the wispy roots. You will need to take out the individual (tiny) bulbs from the outer layer of the base of the plant. The bulbs look like miniature pickled onions but taste more like mild garlic bulbs. They roast down to a creamy nugget of flavour.

1. Preheat the oven to 180°C, 350°F, gas mark 4. Mix together the balsamic vinegar, oil, herbs, sugar and salt in a bowl and let sit for 15 minutes, then taste. The blend should taste like a good balsamic salad dressing; if the liquid is too acidic, add a little more sugar.

2. Add the three-cornered leek bulbs and coat them thoroughly in the vinegary emulsion. Place in an ovenproof dish, cover with a tightly fitting lid, then put in the oven. After 15 minutes check the bulbs – once they have softened to the touch, take them out of the oven. You'll find the skins have hardened, so pop the inside of the bulbs out of their skins and back into the hot dressing. The bulbs are delicious served with salads, on pizza, spread over bread or puréed into a balsamic dipping oil.

TOMATO AND THREE-CORNERED LEEK SOUP

Serves 4

- 250g three-cornered leek stems, coarsely chopped, plus flowers to serve
- Pinch of salt
- 1 tbsp mild olive oil
- 200ml passata
- 4 free-range organic eggs
- 4 slices of bread, such as ciabatta, toasted
- Crumbled goat's cheese or sprinkling of paprika, to serve

This Portuguese-style tomato soup with eggs is delicious with the addition of the native three-cornered leeks.

1. Sweat most of the leek in the oil in a saucepan, reserving a few flowers and stems. When wilted add the salt and passata and cook for 5 minutes, stirring to make sure the leeks do not stick to the bottom of the pan. Add enough water to loosen the mixture, then simmer until slightly reduced and thickening.

2. Carefully crack the eggs onto the soup and keep cooking until the whites are cooked through.

3. To serve, spoon the soup and an egg onto each slice of lightly toasted bread – finish with a sprinkle of chopped leaves or flowers and, if desired, crumble over some goat's cheese or sprinkle with a little paprika.

Leaves grow at the top of flowering and leaf stems, looking slightly similar to elder tree leaves. The leaves are oval and toothed around the edges, with the bottom leaves appearing to split into two. Young leaves can be used in salads, older ones chopped in place of parsley or lovage.

Ground elder has a distinctive carrot family 'umbel' or umbrella-shaped flower head. The main umbel is further divided into several smaller 'umbellets'. Each smaller cluster has 15 to 20 rays (stems) that are each topped with one five-petalled white flower. Unopened buds taste like carrot tops.

Hairless flower stems are circular, hollow and grooved.

Each flower, once pollinated, produces a small slim fruit that ripens into a tiny light-brown edible seed, which can be used as a mild, aromatic spice.

Growing straight from rhizomes in the ground, the hollow leaf stem has a U-shaped groove. Each stem grows only one set of leaves, and when fully grown the stems are around 30cm long. The stems taste like mild celery.

Caution: Be extremely vigilant when gathering any plant within the carrot family; take care to get to know the leaf and stem shapes, the lack of hairs, the perfume of the plant and the shape of flowers and seeds when they form.

GROUND ELDER

Aegopodium podagraria

DISTRIBUTION

Europe, Asia, North America, New Zealand and Australia.

HABITAT

Thriving in damp, slightly shady areas in gardens, woodland verges and pathways.

GATHERING SEASONS

Late winter:
Young glossy leaves, emerging with russet tinges in late winter.

Spring–autumn:
Leaves, flowering stems, flower buds, flowers and seeds. (Re-emerging new tender growth from mowed areas can be harvested until the autumn.)

With its abundant, shade-tolerant, beautiful white umbel flower heads, ground elder would be regarded as a prized early summer-flowering garden plant. If only, that was, it did not have such a frankly well-earned reputation for spreading through gardens like an invading army, colonizing flower beds and dominating weaker plants – just like the Romans, who supposedly spread ground elder through their expanding Empire. Whether they took ground elder with them on their conquests or just made use of an already present plant is unclear, but what is clear is that they used ground elder for both food and its medical prowess. Roman ruling classes showed off their power and wealth with rich diets and feasting which, along with their penchant for using lead cooking pots, resulted in widespread gout amongst the marching armies' leaders. They were so sure that ground elder could cure gout that it earned itself the name 'gout weed'. Eventually, though, gout got the better of the expanded waistline of the Roman Empire, and may even have contributed to its weakening position and inability to defend its conquests from more brutal, stronger armies, falling as fast as it rose.

Just as you might think you've got rid of the invading army of ground elder, diligently pulling up every last spaghetti-like root in your own little kingdom, sure enough it comes back – and just like ground elder, so rule from Rome slowly crept back, this time in the form of the Roman Catholic Church. All across Europe monasteries were established to spread the Christian faith and show off the power and wealth of the Church in Rome, and with the establishment of the monasteries came a resurgence in the spread of ground elder. This was planted in monastic gardens, again to make herbal cures for the age-old affliction of people who want to show off their power; rich and indulgent food which led to yet more gout.

GROUND ELDER

Aside from its historical use in treating gout, ground elder is rich in iron, calcium, magnesium and vitamin C, and when it is younger, the antibacterial essential oil limonene (the same as in lemons). A member of the vast carrot family, its carotene content gives it its distinctive flavour. Ground elder is one of the first spring greens to emerge, so gather the glossy young shoots and leaves when they are tender for salads; later, as they grow taller, they can be used in soups, sauces, herb pies and salads.

ROASTED CARROT AND GROUND ELDER PESTO
Serves 4

- 8 carrots
- 150ml mild olive oil
- 3 tbsp unsalted pistachio nuts
- 1 garlic clove
- 100g ground elder leaves and stems, washed, dried and roughly chopped, flowers and buds reserved
- Juice and zest of 1 lemon
- Salt and freshly ground black pepper
- Sumac and toasted sesame seeds, to serve (optional)

Ground elder leaves are delicious turned into a pesto and served with roasted carrots. You can alternate the ground elder recipe with carrot tops if you are unfortunate enough not to be plagued with ground elder.

1. Preheat the oven to 200°C, 400°F, gas mark 6.

2. Wash the carrots and slice in half lengthways. Toss in 2 tablespoons of the olive oil, season with salt and pepper and place on a baking sheet. Roast for 30–40 minutes until the carrots are caramelized and soft.

3. To make the pesto, process the pistachios and garlic in a food processor until chopped into small pieces. Once they have broken up, add the ground elder, lemon juice and zest, and season with salt and pepper, then add the rest of the olive oil and, if needed, a tablespoon of water to loosen the mix.

4. Serve the pesto over the roasted carrots with a sprinkle of sumac or lemon zest, toasted sesame seeds and a scattering of ground elder flowers.

NEARLY COLUMELLA'S SALAD

Serves 4

- 50g mint leaves and/or pennyroyal, roughly chopped
- 50g coriander leaves, roughly chopped
- 100g ground elder leaves, roughly chopped
- 2 spring onions, roughly chopped
- 200g feta or salted fresh cheese, cut into cubes
- 100ml extra virgin olive oil
- 35ml red wine vinegar
- 1 tsp fresh thyme leaves
- Pinch of pepper

Lucius Columella was a Roman scholar who was fascinated by both wild and cultivated food, writing down recipes for salads that would be as at home in today's meals as they were 2,000 years ago. The original version of this recipe by the gourmet scholar reads like a modern-day chopped salad and included parsley rather than ground elder, but perhaps that was only because he didn't have a flowerbed full to eat?

1. Toss the mint/pennyroyal, coriander, ground elder, onions and feta in the olive oil, vinegar, thyme and pepper. Columella lightly pounded all of his ingredients in a mortar, which the historically correct amongst you may want to do. Serve with chunks of fresh bread.

GROUND ELDER TABBOULEH

Serves 4

- 100g fine bulgur wheat
- 2 medium shallots, finely chopped
- 4 medium tomatoes, diced into 5mm cubes, juice reserved (at room temperature)
- 3–4 tbsp lemon juice
- 120ml top-quality olive oil
- 200g ground elder leaves and stems
- 30g mint leaves
- Salt and freshly ground black pepper

Ground elder leaves and stems make an ideal substitute for the copious amount of parsley required in a proper tabbouleh salad, which should be more leaf than anything else. If you have ground elder growing in your garden it should take no time at all to gather bunches of the delicious herb.

1. Rinse the bulgur wheat in a sieve with cold water until the water runs clear. Cook according to the packet instructions, drain and cool.

2. Mix the bulgur wheat, shallots and tomatoes together with the lemon juice and olive oil. Finely chop the ground elder leaves and stems and mint with a very sharp knife, as finely as possible, then add to the vegetables and bulgur wheat. Season with salt and pepper and serve.

Tightly closed dandelion buds form initially at the base of the stem. Gather them for pickles or to be candied, or fry them and add to salads.

Each flower head is made up of many individual flowers. Containing antioxidants and vitamins A and B12, they can be used in salads and cakes or infused into sugar and water to make a honey-flavoured syrup.

Edible hollow stems.

Growing from a rosette above the taproot, dandelion leaves are hairless, with deep curved notches in the leaf; they can grow up to 30cm in height. Use young leaves as bitter salad herbs.

Caution: Avoid gathering plants treated with herbicides.

Thick taproots can be gathered in autumn and winter, and are traditionally used as a vegetable, roasted or used as a coffee alternative. Dandelion root is rich in inulin, which helps support the growth of healthy bacteria in the gut.

DANDELION

Taraxacum officinale

❧ DISTRIBUTION

Originally native to Europe
and Asia, dandelion is
naturalized in nearly all
temperate parts of the world.

❧ HABITAT

Dandelions are found in
most environments – from
cracks in pavements to the
most manicured lawns.

**❧ GATHERING
SEASONS**

Autumn–spring:
Young leaves and roots.

Spring–summer:
Flowers, flowering stems and
leaves (flowers mainly open
in mid-spring, but can be
found all summer).

If there is one plant that represents our modern-day lack of
understanding of wild food it is dandelion – regarded at best as rabbit
food, at worst as the reason to reach for weedkiller. Each spring many
gardeners wage war on the brightly coloured flowers. They are not
disliked because they are ugly or toxic, but because once the seed
disperses, dandelions will start breeding. Yet allowing dandelions to
thrive leads to huge benefits, not only to feed rabbits (which breed like
dandelions) or people, but in the springtime dandelion provides some
of the earliest, nectar-rich flowers that are vital for, and loved by, bees.

Our current dislike for dandelions is a modern trend; these plants have
been in our diets for thousands of years and probably even longer
than that. As long as there are records of food use there are records of
dandelions being eaten. Dandelions are a nutritional powerhouse: from
prebiotic inulin-rich roots which support gut flora to leaves crammed
with calcium, vitamins A and K, and carotene- and antioxidant-rich
flowers, they help support the liver and kidneys, which in turn support
healthy hormone levels, flush the body of toxins and support healthy
bone formation. They are beautiful, useful and incredibly easy to grow,
so it's time for dandelion lawns to make a comeback.

DANDELION

From the roots to the flowers, all parts of dandelions are edible. Some parts are sweet, others intensely bitter, but all are intensely flavoured and equally good for you. Gather roots in the autumn and winter, steam for a few minutes and the outer skin will slip off, or roast as a vegetable, glazed in honey. Dried and roasted roots are excellent infused into bitters, cream desserts, chai and to make dandelion coffee.

SAUTÉED DANDELIONS – HINBEH
Serves 4

- 200g dandelion greens (a colander full)
- 100ml extra virgin olive oil
- 4 medium onions, thinly sliced
- Salt, to taste
- Lemon wedges, to serve
- Chilli flakes, to serve (optional)

Dandelions are still a staple in parts of Europe and the Middle East and many countries have their own version of a sautéed dandelion dish. This version originates from the Levant, an area where people still eat many wild foods, inspired by the wild larder of their nomadic ancestors.

1. Thoroughly wash and drain the dandelion greens. Trim the bottoms of the stalks and coarsely chop. Fill a large pan with water and bring to the boil over a medium–high heat. Add salt to taste then add the dandelions. Bring back to the boil and cook for 5 minutes. Drain the dandelions and dunk them in a bowl of iced water. Drain the cooked greens in a colander and squeeze out as much liquid as you can.

2. Add the olive oil to a frying pan over a medium heat and fry the onions, stirring occasionally, until they turn a rich golden brown. Remove half of the onions with a slotted spoon and allow them to drain on several layers of kitchen roll. Add the dandelion leaves to the remaining fried onions in the pan. Sauté over a medium heat for a couple of minutes, stirring regularly until the greens and onions are mixed.

3. Leave to cool before serving at room temperature, with a squeeze of lemon and garnished with the crispy onions. If you would like a little heat, sprinkle over some chilli flakes.

DANDELION FUGAZZA CAKE

Serves 4–6

- 25g fresh yeast or 7g dried yeast
- 120g butter, softened
- 100ml lukewarm milk
- Pinch of salt
- 500g plain flour
- 2 tsp vanilla sugar
- 160g sugar
- Grated zest of 1 lemon
- 10g dandelion petals
- 2 eggs
- 2 tbsp granulated sugar

Easter baking in the Veneto region of northeastern Italy includes fugazza yeast cake, and the addition of dandelion petals is a delicious nod to the bright fields of *brusaoci*.

1. Dissolve the yeast in a bowl of lukewarm milk and leave for 10 minutes or until the yeast starts foaming. Sift half the flour into the liquid and stir to make a batter. Cover with a damp tea towel and leave in a warm place for 30 minutes or until the mixture has doubled its size.

2. When doubled in size, mix in the remaining ingredients, pulling them together into a soft dough. Knead for 5 minutes (add more flour if the dough is too sticky), then place the dough in a greased 20cm cake tin, cover with a damp tea towel and leave to rise until doubled in size.

3. Preheat the oven to 170°C, 325°F, gas mark 3.

4. Sprinkle the dough with the granulated sugar and bake for 30 minutes until golden. Serve with yoghurt or cream.

DANDELION ROOT COFFEE AFFOGATO – (DROWNED ICE CREAM)

Makes a 250g jar of ground dandelion root coffee

- 6 large dandelion roots, washed and finely diced
- Vanilla ice cream
- Chocolate shavings or nuts, to serve

Roasted dandelion roots have the depth and body of coffee, and also contain prebiotics, which are important for gut and immune health. A strong brew of dandelion coffee served over vanilla ice cream balances the virtuous and indulgent books.

1. Preheat the oven to 120°C, 250°F, gas mark ½.

2. Spread out the diced roots on baking trays and put in the oven; the roots will slowly turn a dark brown colour, which can take a couple of hours – regularly check that they are not burning, and move the roots around if they are not roasting evenly. Remove from the oven and let cool, then grind in a coffee grinder and store in a glass jar.

3. To make the coffee, use 2 teaspoons per cup of just-boiled water in a cafetière. To serve with the ice cream, make a stronger coffee – 4 teaspoons per cup. Spoon the coffee over balls of ice cream, finishing with chocolate shavings or nuts.

SORREL

Rumex acetosa

◉ DISTRIBUTION

Native to Europe, North
Africa and Asia, introduced
to America.

◉ HABITAT

Moist grassland, meadows
and lawns.

**◉ GATHERING
SEASONS**

Early autumn–late spring:
Young tender leaves.

Late spring–midsummer:
Flowering stem and
flowers/seeds.

The naming of plants often gives clues to their uses throughout history. Sorrel is no exception; sorrel and acetosa stem from the French word *surele*, meaning sour, and Italian *acetosa*, meaning vinegary – 'sour and vinegary', perhaps the most perfect description for the flavour and long use of the little acidic wild plant that grows at most of our feet.

With long taproots, sorrel pulls up vast amounts of vitamins C and A alongside sodium, potassium, magnesium, calcium and iron. Tasting like a combination of sour apple, lime and lemon, sorrel provides delicious sourness to both sweet and savoury dishes alike. Sorrel has been eaten as a vegetable for over 4,000 years; its sourness crops up in recipes as frequently as it does in grassland and it is one of the most common wild plants growing in grasslands across Europe and Asia. From lawns to meadows, crouch down and look for clusters of young, vibrant green leaves looking like blunt arrowheads – where you find one you'll be sure to find more, and once you've nibbled a leaf you'll definitely want to eat more.

Wide rounded leaves with pointed tails, becoming longer and more like an arrowhead as they grow.

Caution: Take care not to misidentify with poisonous Lords and Ladies (arum lily), whose leaves are glossier, paler underneath, with protruding, branched veins. Sorrel leaves are more silken, with pointed tails.

Sorrel contains oxalic acid, which is present in many foods, from spinach to rhubarb, but is best avoided by people with kidney function issues.

Small red, cream and green flowers that mature to contain seeds. The young flowers are powdery and dry with a mild, lemony flavour.

Pectin-rich and acidic tender stems can be added to salads, tougher stems blitzed to extract their sour juice for cocktails and dressings.

COOK & EAT
SORREL

Sorrel featured in the first published French cookbook as an ingredient to cut through the strong flavour of pike; 700 years later, it is still an important herb in European, African and Asian food. Sorrel can be used raw or cooked in sweet and savoury food, making it a valuable and versatile ingredient. Sorrel's sharpness cuts through the richness of egg or cream, oily fish and fatty meats.

SORREL DAL
Serves 4

- 4 tsp vegetable oil
- 1 tsp mustard seeds
- ½ tsp cumin seeds
- 100g yellow split peas, soaked for 30 minutes
- 1 red chilli, thinly sliced
- 2 onions, 1 finely diced, 1 finely sliced
- 3 garlic cloves, crushed
- Powdered spice mix of ½ tsp cumin, ½ tsp turmeric, ½ tsp fenugreek powder
- 50g sorrel leaves and stems
- 30g fresh coriander
- Salt

Forms of sorrel are widely used in Indian cooking, especially in northern India, where it is added to dals, curries, rice, pickles, chutneys and sauces. Its sourness echoes tamarind and lime and can be swapped in place of either in many recipes. Adding at the end of cooking as a fresh herb gives a refreshing tang to nourishing dal.

1. Heat 3 tsp of the oil and toast the mustard and cumin seeds for 1 minute, stirring continually. Add the split peas, chilli, garlic, finely diced onion and double the amount of water as volume of the peas. Place on a high heat, and bring to a hard boil before turning down and simmering until the dal is soft, usually 40–50 minutes (older pulses can take longer to soften). Stir regularly to make sure the dal does not burn on the bottom of the pan.

2. In a separate pan, heat the remaining oil and add the finely sliced onion, cooking until the onion becomes browned and crisp. When the dal is softened, stir in the powdered spice mix and cook on a gentle heat for 10 further minutes. Stir in the sorrel, coriander leaves and salt to taste. Top with the crisped onions, and serve with rice or bread.

SORREL SALSA VERDE
Makes 200g

- 50g sorrel
- 25g rocket or bittercress
- 25g spinach or chickweed
- 25g mint leaves
- 25g spring onions, chives or three-cornered leek
- 25g parsley or ground elder
- 100ml cider vinegar or white wine vinegar
- 2 tsp sugar
- 1 tsp salt
- 100ml light olive oil

Bartolomeo Scappi was the first celebrity chef, cooking for the rich, royals and papal parties in the sixteenth century. In his recipe book *The Opera of Bartolomeo Scappi*, he used sorrel in salads and salsa verde (green sauce). He recommended that it be used to complement a 'Roe Deer that is a yearling in life'. Salsa verde does indeed taste wonderful with venison of any age, but it also tastes pretty sensational drizzled over potato salads, or dolloped on bread and cheese.

1. Finely chop the herbs either by hand or in a food processor until you have a coarse blend. Place the chopped herbs in a bowl and add half of the vinegar, 1 teaspoon of sugar and ½ teaspoon of salt. Stir all the ingredients together and leave to macerate for 5 minutes before tasting; if the vinegar is overpowering add more sugar, if too sweet add a pinch more salt. Add more vinegar if required to loosen the mixture, and finish by lightly whisking in the olive oil. Store in the fridge for up to a week.

SORREL AND APPLE VERJUS (GREEN JUICE)
Makes 250ml

- 100g sorrel leaves and stalks
- 250ml unsweetened apple juice (the sourest you can buy)

Verjus is made with the juice of unripe fruit, an ancient ingredient that is thought to have been originally made with sorrel juice blended with the sour fruit. Verjus is an unfermented alternative to vinegar; traditionally used when drinking wine with a meal, it is said to open taste buds, unlike vinegar, which tightens them. It can be used to dress salads, to provide acidity to oily dishes and to make ice lollies and granitas.

1. In a juicer, blend the sorrel leaves and stalks with the apple juice. Strain and keep in the fridge for up to two weeks or freeze in ice-cube trays until required. (You can put the leftover pulp into a jar and cover with vodka for 24 hours to extract the sour flavour into the alcohol, or cover with apple cider vinegar to infuse sorrel flavour into the vinegar.)

2. Sorrel pairs incredibly well with young pine or spruce tips and elderflower. To turn your verjus into a sensationally vibrant cocktail, shake 100ml of the verjus with 10ml elderflower cordial, the juice of 1 lime and 30ml vodka. Lengthen with apple juice or serve on the sourest of rocks.

NETTLE

Urtica spp.

● DISTRIBUTION

Forms of nettle grow across
most areas of the world,
except for arid regions.

● HABITAT

Nitrogen-rich damp soils, in
open sun or shade.

**● GATHERING
SEASONS**

Early spring–mid-winter:
Nettle leaves from plants
before they have flowered.

Summer–autumn:
Green seeds.

Nettles grow in fertile soils, thriving in places where people and animals have left their nitrogen-rich mark. As a result, wherever people live, nettles often grow – colonizing flower beds and creating tinglingly painful thickets at the back of gardens. There is no escaping the fact that a brush with nettle is unpleasant, but when the plant's value is realized, even the sting might appear less irritating. For thousands of years people have gathered the plant for food and medicine; a plant that is worth the risk of such discomfort must have something about it, and nettles really do.

Nettles are one of the most nutritious, complete foods on the planet. Yellow rope-like roots spread through the ground with an extraordinary ability to pull up nutrients, including trace elements such as boron, an element found in the soil but created in the far more cosmic setting of space. Absorbed into the Earth's atmosphere, it plays a vital role in supporting plant growth, and is equally vital for human health, supporting bone density and muscle strength and preventing osteoporosis. Nettle's ability to draw whatever is in the soil makes it one of the easiest ways to get the important element into our bodies. Along with providing trace elements, the sting-laden plants are also a rich source of vitamins A and C, iron, potassium and numerous other minerals, and the equally mineral-dense seeds provide a late-summer adrenal boost. Sweeteners that soften the sting of nettles lie within the irritating hairs themselves. The hypodermic needles release formic acid, histamine and other chemicals that may be painful at the time, but stimulate circulation and fight inflammation. And if you do happen to get stung by a nettle, the plant has a final offering for you; grinding the leaves releases a juice full of histamine blockers, which when applied to tingling skin, soothes their own stings away.

Emerging from where leaf stems join the main plant stem, tiny green and white flowers grow along short stems. The flowers ripen into green seeds that surround the stem like jewellery beads. Nettle seeds are nutritionally rich and energy-giving and support the adrenal system. Rubbed through a sieve to break down any stings, the seeds can be eaten raw and added to food and drinks.

Nettle's square stems produce jagged-edged, heart-shaped leaves which decrease in size as they reach the tip of the plant, and these tip leaves are the ones to gather. Don gloves and collect from young plants before they have flowered to use in savoury and sweet dishes.

Caution: Avoid gathering nettles from roadsides or anywhere with contaminated soil, and only gather the nettle leaves from young plants before they have produced flowers. Nettle stings usually result in mild irritation, but very occasionally people can be seriously allergic.

Urtica dioica

NETTLE

Nettle emerges in and tastes of spring; minerally and grassy, the young tips can be used in a wide range of savoury and sweet dishes. Traditionally eaten in spring to warm the blood after winter, young leaves can be gathered from spring until hard winter frosts, if your patch of nettles has an occasional strim. Autumn often brings a second flush of growth; gather the top leaves, wilt and squeeze into balls to freeze.

NETTLE SPANAKOPITA
Serves 4

- 200g nettle tips
- 30g mint leaves
- 1 tbsp light olive oil
- 1 large onion, finely chopped
- 1 garlic clove, grated
- Zest of 1 organic lemon
- ¼ tsp grated nutmeg
- 2 free-range organic eggs, beaten
- 300g ricotta
- 100g feta cheese, crumbled
- 8 sheets of filo pastry
- Melted butter, for brushing
- Sesame seeds, for scattering
- Salt and freshly ground black pepper

Nettles have a long association with Greek food and medicine. Greek wild greens (*horta*), are often added to pies encased in filo pastry, or topped with a gluten-free cornmeal crust (known as *pispilita*). Filo or cornmeal, these pies are utterly delicious eaten warm or cold.

1. Plunge the nettle tips into boiling water for a minute. Immediately strain them, and when cooled, finely chop with the mint leaves and place in a large mixing bowl. Heat the oil in a pan and sweat the onion until soft and translucent, adding the garlic, lemon zest and nutmeg, and seasoning with salt and pepper. Mix the onion mixture and eggs with the nettle and mint; finally stir in the ricotta and crumbled feta cheese.

2. Preheat the oven to 160°C, 325°F, gas mark 3.

3. Brush four sheets of filo pastry with some melted butter and lay them on top of one another on a baking tray. Spoon the filling onto the pastry. Cover with another four buttered filo sheets and roll the ends together to seal the pie. Sprinkle with sesame seeds and bake for 40 minutes or until golden. Serve with a green salad.

NETTLE AND ELDERFLOWER HAYFEVER TEA

Makes 1 cup

- 5–6 nettle leaves
- 1 tsp fresh elderflowers
  (or ½ flower head)

Histamine in nettle binds to receptors in our bodies to temporarily block production of our own histamine – which is good news for hayfever sufferers. This simple tea, pairing nettle with elderflower (which contains quercetin, a natural antihistamine), is not only a refreshing summer tea but is also known to help reduce symptoms of hayfever. If you are out and have a hayfever attack, pushing nettles and elderflowers into your drinks bottle and leaving for a few minutes to infuse will work too; just remember to remove the nettles before you drink from the bottle!

1. Place the nettle leaves and the fresh elderflowers (pulled off their stalks) in a mug and add freshly boiled water. Cover and leave for 5–10 minutes, then drink. Take three to four times a day. It is worth drinking this tea as soon as the first elderflowers open, even if your hayfever symptoms haven't started, to help prevent an attack.

NETTLE CUPCAKES

Makes 12

- 75g nettles
- 100g plain yoghurt
- Zest and juice of 1 lemon
- 120g butter
- 120g sugar
- 2 free-range organic eggs
- 250g self-raising flour
- 1 tsp baking powder

Pistachio-green nettle cakes are a sweet way of eating vegetables. Even greens-hating children devour nettles in cake form.

1. Preheat the oven to 120°C, 250°F, gas mark ½.

2. Plunge the nettles into a bowl of boiling water for 30 seconds, straining them immediately into a bowl of ice-cold water. Squeeze out the water from the leaves and blend in a food processor with the yoghurt, lemon zest and juice until smooth. In another bowl, cream the butter and sugar, and slowly add the eggs, flour and baking powder. Fold together and finally add the nettle/yoghurt mix.

3. Pour into muffin cases and bake for 20–25 minutes or until the cakes bounce back when gently pressed.

HERB BENNET

Geum urbanum

● DISTRIBUTION

Europe, Middle East, Russia,
Central Asia, North America
and New Zealand.

● HABITAT

Herb bennet grows in
shady places, on the edge of
woodland, near shaded ponds
and riversides, in cities and
rural areas alike.

**● GATHERING
SEASONS**

All year:
Roots.

Winter–mid-spring:
Young leaves.

Herb bennet is an unassuming plant. Wiry stems grow almost
indistinguishably through other plants, their modest flowers and little
seedheads almost trying to hide from view, weaving their way through
shady spots of gardens and woodlands. But the coy flowers and
seedheads lead down to a prized treasure hidden under the ground –
roots that smell and taste like exotic cloves. The spiced flavour comes
from eugenol, a chemical produced by a number of plants including
cloves, basil, allspice and cinnamon – very different plants making the
same chemical to protect their tender leaves, fruits and flowers, or in
herb bennet's case, roots. Eugenol is an antifungal and antibacterial
defence within plants, and for hundreds of years we have made use of
the plant for everything from soothing stomach upsets, to reducing
catarrh and treating venomous bites and poisoned wounds. Christian
monks wore the plant around their necks as an amulet to scare away
the devil and other evils. Herbalists today are less likely to tie a root
necklace around your neck, but they will prescribe the antiseptic and
anti-inflammatory herb bennet to treat stomach complaints, gum
disease and mouth ulcers.

As an easily found plant with a wide range of medicinal uses, the
eugenol-rich flavour of herb bennet roots would have been familiar
to many people in the past. Whilst the wealthiest spiced their food
with vastly expensive imported cloves, the majority used the far
more local and free herb bennet roots to spice apples, preserve beer
and flavour liqueurs – it even made the list of ingredients in the first
amaretto. Perhaps the devil doesn't like warming spices, but people
certainly do.

The flowers are followed by
masses of simple fruits, growing
in a cluster to form a rounded
head, which matures into small
burrs with tiny red hooks.

Divided into lobed, rounded
segments, spring leaves growing
at the base of the plant can be
eaten in salads or wilted and
added to soups.

Very small yellow flowers grow at the end of
thin stems, looking like miniature buttercups.
Each flower has five petals, sat on top of pointed,
turned-back green sepals that create a star-like
image under the flower. The flowers bloom all
summer and autumn.

Long, thin, wiry stems growing
up to 60cm tall. Long side stems
produce a branched effect,
ending in a single flower, often
growing between other plants.

The 2.5–5cm-long stubby rhizomes
send out numerous light-brown, fibrous,
clove-scented roots, which give it its
common name, 'clove root'. Unlike cloves,
the roots are not overpowering in flavour.
Best gathered in late winter/early spring
for use as a spice.

HERB BENNET

Young leaves can be eaten raw in salads, tasting mild and slightly nutty, but when they become tough they are best sweated with oil or butter as a vegetable, or added to soups. Dried leaves can be powdered and added to soups or blended with salt for a mild seasoning.

The aromatic roots are best dried and kept away from light and ground as they are needed, infused into syrups or frozen to preserve their scent. Herb bennet warms everything from béchamel sauces to apple pies.

HERB BENNET APPLE PIE
Serves 6–8

- 650g cooking apples
- 50g caster sugar, plus extra for sprinkling
- Knob of butter
- A whole herb bennet root, washed (dried or fresh)
- 250g Shortcrust pastry
- Flour, for dusting
- Milk, for glazing

The first English cookery books record the use of herb bennet as an ingredient for spicing apples. It's a pairing that has stood the test of time and it is a particularly comforting combination in autumn.

1. Finely slice the apples and coat in the sugar before placing them in the bottom of a pie dish. Add 1 tablespoon of water and a knob of butter. Lay the root, spread out like the spokes of a wheel, on top of the pie, with the centre of the root sitting in the middle of the pie.

2. Roll out the pastry on a lightly floured work surface to the size of the pie dish, then place over the apples, pressing it onto the edge of the dish. Cut a small hole in the centre of the pastry, and pull the top of the centre of the roots through the hole. Glaze the lid with milk, sprinkle with a little sugar and chill in the fridge for 30 minutes.

3. Preheat the oven to 200°C, 400°F, gas mark 6. Bake the pie in the oven for 40 minutes. When cooked, pull the whole root out of the pie pastry, leaving behind a clove-scented pie to serve with ice cream or custard.

HERB BENNET ZABAGLIONE

Serves 4

- Roots of 2 herb bennet plants, washed and dried
- 80ml amaretto
- 6 large free-range organic egg yolks
- 2 tbsp caster sugar
- 60ml whipping cream

Herb bennet adds a gentle spiced warmth to zabaglione custards. Herb bennet was one of the original flavours in amaretto and here it is reunited with the liqueur in this light-as-air custard. Delicious served with fresh blackberries, poached pears or roasted rhubarb.

1. Chop the herb bennet roots into small pieces and infuse in the amaretto for two days. Strain the amaretto into a jug, discarding the roots.

2. Whisk the egg yolks, infused amaretto and sugar in a heatproof bowl, place over a saucepan of simmering water or in a bain-marie and cook, whisking continuously for about 5 minutes. Remove the bowl from the pan, add the cream and whisk it into the custard mixture.

3. Serve immediately or chill in the fridge to serve cold.

HERB BENNET-INFUSED BRAISED RED CABBAGE

Serves 6

- 25g butter or lardo, plus 2 tbsp
- ½ large red cabbage, cored and thinly sliced
- 1 large onion, thinly sliced
- 1 large tart apple, cored and grated
- 150ml dry red wine
- 75ml red wine vinegar
- 1 tsp ground cinnamon
- 3 whole herb bennet roots, washed (dried or fresh)
- 1 tbsp brown sugar
- Salt and freshly ground black pepper

Herb bennet roots can be left whole to flavour recipes such as braised red cabbage – just remember to search for them before serving.

1. Heat the butter or lardo in a large pan and add the cabbage, onion and apple and stir well. Add the rest of the ingredients with 600ml water and bring to a boil before reducing to a simmer and cooking until the cabbage is tender, about 1 hour.

2. Remove the herb bennet roots before serving.

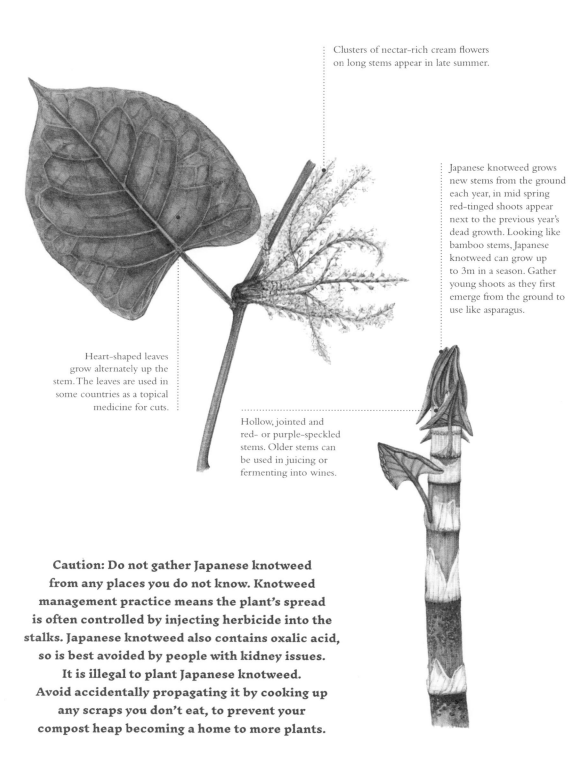

Clusters of nectar-rich cream flowers on long stems appear in late summer.

Japanese knotweed grows new stems from the ground each year, in mid spring red-tinged shoots appear next to the previous year's dead growth. Looking like bamboo stems, Japanese knotweed can grow up to 3m in a season. Gather young shoots as they first emerge from the ground to use like asparagus.

Heart-shaped leaves grow alternately up the stem. The leaves are used in some countries as a topical medicine for cuts.

Hollow, jointed and red- or purple-speckled stems. Older stems can be used in juicing or fermenting into wines.

Caution: Do not gather Japanese knotweed from any places you do not know. Knotweed management practice means the plant's spread is often controlled by injecting herbicide into the stalks. Japanese knotweed also contains oxalic acid, so is best avoided by people with kidney issues. It is illegal to plant Japanese knotweed. Avoid accidentally propagating it by cooking up any scraps you don't eat, to prevent your compost heap becoming a home to more plants.

JAPANESE KNOTWEED

Reynoutria japonica

Japanese knotweed strikes fear into the hearts of homeowners across Europe and America, cursed as being such a rampant invasive so keen to take over the land that it will even grow through tarmac and invade houses. Yes, it does possess super strength, but take a moment to consider its virtues and you might start to view the thicket at the end of your road with less fear.

Japanese knotweed's native residency is high in the mountainous regions of East Asia. Occupying volcanic areas, it plays an important role in regreening lava-covered mountains. Its roots and shoots push through thick blackened rocks, dying back each year and breaking down into a rich layer of mulch, which allows tender seeds to germinate and grow. Slowly, with the help of Japanese knotweed, the black lava bed turns lush green, ecologically diverse and vibrant.

Japanese knotweed's reputation often comes from the fact that it forms thickets of dense planting; part of the reason it does this is because it grows where other plants cannot; just as it shoots upwards, so knotweed plunges downwards. Whether on volcanic mountains or polluted wasteland, Japanese knotweed's taproots can grow down many metres to locate nutrients buried in the subsoil. Japanese knotweed's searching roots are so adept at pulling up whatever is in the ground that they will also draw up toxins and heavy metals, cleaning the earth of contaminants. This remarkable invasive plant re-establishes life above it, cleaning the ground below it.

A member of the Polygonaceae family, Japanese knotweed tastes like rhubarb with a more savoury edge. And, just like its remarkable ability to restore health to soil, the plant is equally nourishing to people, containing high levels of phytonutrients and resveratrol, a polyphenol that supports heart health and provides protection to the ageing brain. The invader at the back of your garden may be less scary than it seems.

JAPANESE KNOTWEED

With the flavours of a mineral-rich rhubarb, Japanese knotweed can be used in sweet and savoury dishes alike. In Japan it is used as a spring vegetable – the young stems are often sautéed, stir-fried, fermented, tempura-ed, pickled or preserved in salt or soy. With the addition of sugar or honey and lemon juice, knotweed can be turned into cordials and wines, juiced for its sour flavour in cocktails, or gently softened and added to jams, jellies, sorbets or crumbles.

JAPANESE KNOTWEED AND LEMON FOOL
Serves 4

- 450g tender Japanese knotweed stems, roughly chopped
- Zest and juice of 1 organic lemon
- 75g sugar
- 300ml double cream
- 100ml Greek yoghurt
- Shiso or lemon balm leaves (optional)

Foods like cream, that are rich in calcium, help reduce the amount of oxalic acid that can be absorbed into your body, making indulgent fools just that bit better for you.

1. Place the knotweed in a pan, add 2 tablespoons of water, the lemon zest and juice and sugar, cover and gently cook until tender. Reserving the juice, drain the knotweed, stirring in more sugar, if required, and leave to cool.

2. In another bowl, whip the cream to soft peaks and gently fold in the yoghurt and cooled knotweed. Chill for at least an hour. Serve with some of the juice drizzled over the top, and scatter over the shiso or lemon balm leaves, if using.

SALTED ITADORI

Makes around 150g

....

- 250g young knotweed shoots
- 60g sea salt

....

In Japan, knotweed is preserved in salt. This traditional method is used to both remove oxalic acid and preserve the vegetable for later use.

1. Peel the knotweed and cut it into 5cm lengths. Place the shoots in a bowl and add 50g of the salt, rubbing it into the knotweed. Pack the salt-covered shoots into a tupperware container. The salt should start drawing out liquid from the shoots. Check every day that the knotweed is under the salty liquid and place a weight (or bag filled with water) on top to ensure it is fully submerged.

2. After ten days, strain the shoots and discard the salty liquid. Return the knotweed to the tupperware, sprinkling the remaining 10g of salt between each layer, then placing the weight back on the knotweed to ensure it is covered by any liquid that comes out. Store in an airtight container in a cool, dry place until needed.

3. To use, remove the salt by soaking in a few of changes of water before eating raw or cooking.

ROASTED JAPANESE KNOTWEED SHOOTS IN MISO AND SOY

Serves 4

....

- 1 tbsp miso paste
- 1 tbsp dark soy sauce
- Thumb-sized piece of fresh root ginger, grated
- 1 garlic clove, grated
- 400g young knotweed shoots
- Vegetable oil, to drizzle

....

Young emerging Japanese knotweed shoots are delicious roasted or griddled. Roasting with a coating of miso and soy creates a sticky, sour vegetable.

1. Preheat the oven to 180°C, 350°F, gas mark 4.

2. Mix together the miso, soy, ginger and garlic into a paste in a bowl. Wash and trim the shoots, discarding any tough ends. Toss them in the paste, and drizzle with vegetable oil.

3. Place in the oven and roast for 20–25 minutes or until tender.

WILD GARLIC

Allium spp.

Wild garlic is commonly known in many countries as bear's garlic,
due to the appetite that newly woken bears have for it in spring. A
well-chosen post-hibernation feast, wild garlic not only tastes good,
but is also rich in antibacterial and antibiotic properties. The pungent
leaves containing vitamins A and C are rich in iron and calcium
and also contain trace elements of phosphorous, sodium and copper.
Like other forms of garlic, wild garlic has been shown in studies to
improve heart health and lower blood pressure.

In late winter, the young leaves soon grow to carpet woodland floors.
Long spear-shaped leaves with a single central vein seamlessly grow
from almost-white stems that emerge straight from the ground in
clusters from closely grouped bulbs. Flower stems grow from the
centre of the plant with a closed, pointed flower bud which eventually
grows taller than the leaves. When the warm weather arrives, the stem
opens to reveal a globe of white, star-like flowers, followed by small
green fruits ripening into black seeds. All parts of wild garlic are edible
and delicious, but avoid uprooting the plants to gather the bulbs –
especially in places where wild garlic is not abundant.

When wild garlic is abundant it is tempting to gather handfuls of the
leaves, but it should be harvested with care, as there are poisonous
lookalike plants which grow in the same habitat, including lily of
the valley and the deadly autumn crocus. Smell alone isn't enough to
distinguish these plants, so collect leaf by leaf rather than ripping up
handfuls. Until you are totally confident of your finds, gather wild
garlic when the flowers have started to open, as this will provide an
extra level of certainty that you are picking the right plant; autumn
crocus flowers later in the year, and lily of the valley has bell-shaped
white flowers quite distinct from wild garlic. After a careful foray you
will be rewarded with leaves, flowers and seeds that can be used fresh
or transformed into sensational flavouring for the year ahead.

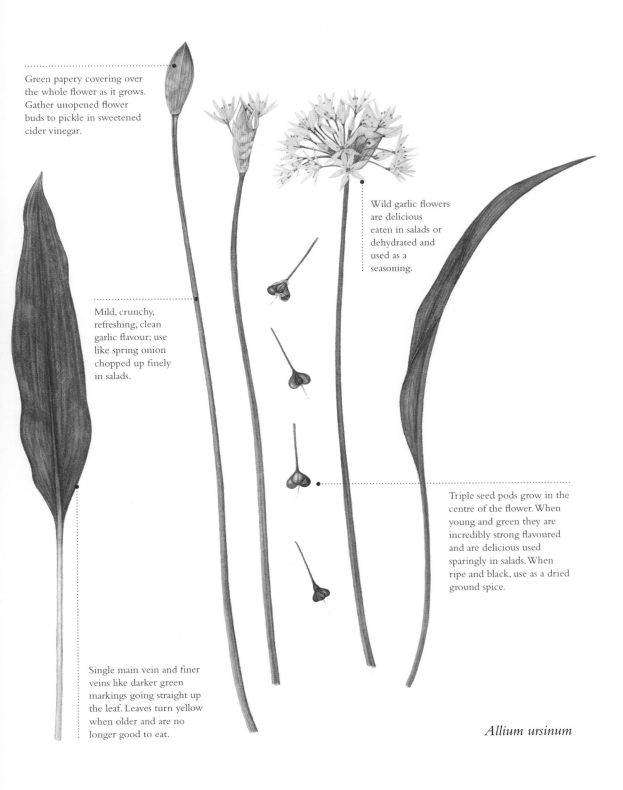

Green papery covering over the whole flower as it grows. Gather unopened flower buds to pickle in sweetened cider vinegar.

Mild, crunchy, refreshing, clean garlic flavour; use like spring onion chopped up finely in salads.

Wild garlic flowers are delicious eaten in salads or dehydrated and used as a seasoning.

Triple seed pods grow in the centre of the flower. When young and green they are incredibly strong flavoured and are delicious used sparingly in salads. When ripe and black, use as a dried ground spice.

Single main vein and finer veins like darker green markings going straight up the leaf. Leaves turn yellow when older and are no longer good to eat.

Allium ursinum

WILD GARLIC

All parts of the wild garlic plant are edible, and all have different textures and flavours – from mild flower stems to powerfully hot seedheads. Gather unopened flower buds to pickle in sweetened cider vinegar, and use the edible flowers to add colour and flavour to salads and in salting. The stems have a mild, crunchy, clean garlic flavour and can be used like spring onion.

Freshly gathered wild garlic transforms risottos, frittatas, soups and salads, and when wilted with butter it makes a delicious alternative to spinach.

SALTED WILD GARLIC FLOWERS
Makes 25g dried flowers

- 1 litre hot water
- 60g salt
- 125g wild garlic flowers

Brining and drying wild garlic flowers creates an umami-rich seasoning that sits alongside salt and pepper as an essential flavouring in wild kitchens. It is sensational in soups and dips and on breads, vegetables, and meats. (You can swap the flowers in this recipe for leaves, buds, or flowering stems; each part of the wild garlic plant has a slightly different flavour but all are delicious in salt.)

1. Dissolve the salt in the hot water and leave to cool. Rinse the flowers, then place them in the brine. To ensure the wild garlic is fully submerged in the brine, press a small, clean plate into the liquid, to push the flowers down. Leave at room temperature for 2 days (during which time your kitchen will fill with wild garlic perfume). Drain the wild garlic then wrap it in a tea towel and squeeze out any remaining liquid. Place the damp wild garlic onto a clean dry cloth and dry over a radiator or in a dehydrator on its lowest setting.

2. When the wild garlic is totally dry it will be easy to crumble – rub it into a coarse powder and place in airtight jars to store for up to a year.

SOY AND WILD GARLIC SAUCE
Makes 150g

- 50g wild garlic leaves and flowering stems
- Sesame oil, to coat
- 50ml soy sauce
- 10g unrefined sugar
- 30ml rice wine vinegar
- Thumb-sized piece of fresh root ginger, finely grated
- Pinch of red chilli flakes
- Toasted sesame seeds, to finish

The species of wild garlic that grows in Korea is highly prized and often blended with soy sauce to create kimchi, or is served freshly braised. Ready to use instantly, warm or cold, this sauce is delicious over fried eggs and rice, or puréed as a marinade for pork.

1. Finely chop the wild garlic leaves and flowering stems (these give crunch and texture). Stir through enough sesame oil to coat and set to one side while you make the dressing.

2. Put the soy sauce, sugar and 50ml water into a small pan, bring the mixture to a boil over a medium heat and then immediately take off the heat. Add the rice wine vinegar, ginger and a pinch of red chilli flakes. Mix together well, before pouring over the wild garlic leaves and stems. Finish with a sprinkling of toasted sesame seeds.

3. If you are not using this immediately, transfer to a sealed jar and store in the fridge, where it will keep for up to a week.

WILD GARLIC AND NETTLE PISTOU
Makes 250g

- 100g wild garlic leaves
- 50g nettle leaves
- 100ml light olive oil
- Juice of 1 lemon
- Pinch each of salt and sugar
- ½ tsp mustard powder

In season at the same time and found growing in the same locations, nettle lends wild garlic an iron-rich depth and roundness of flavour when the two are combined. They are perfect companions in springtime sauces such as a French pistou, or you can turn this into a wild garlic pesto with the addition of 50g ground nuts and 50g finely grated hard cheese.

1. Plunge the cleaned wild garlic and nettle leaves into a pan of boiling water for 10 seconds. Take them out of the water and transfer them straight into a bowl of ice-cold water. Drain, then squeeze out the remaining liquid. Roughly chop the leaves before placing them in a food processor with the olive oil, the lemon juice, a pinch of salt and sugar, and the mustard powder. Blend to a coarse purée, taste and add extra seasoning if required.

2. If you are not using this immediately, transfer to a sealed jar and store in the fridge, where it will keep for up to 10 days, or up to 6 months in the freezer.

DOCK

Rumex spp.

❧ DISTRIBUTION

Global.

❧ HABITAT

Docks grow in most
environments, from rich,
fertile garden borders
to nutrient-poor, stony
wasteland.

**❧ GATHERING
SEASONS**

Late winter–early spring:
Roots and young shoots and
leaves.

Mid-spring–autumn:
Larger but tender-looking
leaves and stems.

Summer–early autumn:
Seeds.

People are almost born with the knowledge of what a dock looks
like; from their first nettle sting the large, oval, bright green leaves
are searched out instinctively, and with utter relief a rub of the leaf
will soothe away the pain. Fortunately, it doesn't usually take long to
find a dock leaf, one of the most common and widespread plants in
the world, whose success lies in the ability to grow in even the most
over-grazed and stony land.

Dock's ability to thrive anywhere has led to it being regarded as
a noxious weed, yet it is far from that. Thanks to its thick orange
taproots, which push deep into the ground, pulling up huge amounts
of nourishment from the subsoil, docks are packed full of goodness
in a volume that cultivated greens like spinach can only bow down
to. The leaves and stems – rich in vitamin C, iron, minerals, and trace
elements of phosphate, potassium and magnesium – wither back and
die each year, returning their nutrition to the topsoil, nourishing the
often-depleted ground. Docks are far more useful than just being
used for soothing stings...

What of its legendary cure of nettle sting? Does rubbing a dock leaf
on your skin work? Rubbing a leaf on your pin-pricked leg won't
help other than as a placebo, but what is useful is the slippery gel-like
substance found in the *stems* of young leaves in the base of the plant –
not just for stings but also for burns and bites.

Up to 50cm long, dock leaves
have a crimpled-looking edge.
The central vein has a sour
flavour; green parts of young
leaves taste slightly bitter.

Stems rich in pectin.
Tender stems have a sour,
savoury bite – delicious
chopped into salads and
on seafood.

Bright yellow/orange
taproot rich in minerals
and iron. Used in herbal
tinctures and bitters.

Flower stalks can grow to 1 metre;
green/pink flowers develop rusty
coloured mineral-rich seeds. The
seeds can be ground and used as a
mineral supplement.

DOCK

Part of the Polygonaceae family, which includes rhubarb and sorrel, dock contains oxalic acid (perfectly safe in moderation, but best avoided if you have kidney complaints), which gives it a sour flavour. But unlike its fruity siblings, dock has a more savoury, vegetable and bitter taste, which makes it an ideal swap for greens such as spinach, kale and chard.

DOCK DOLMA
Makes 20 small or 10 large dolma

- 100g green lentils
- 25g rice
- 1 medium onion, finely chopped
- 20g raisins, coarsely chopped
- 20g sun-dried tomatoes, coarsely chopped
- 20g pistachios (or pine nuts), coarsely chopped
- A bunch of fennel, oregano or dill, finely chopped
- 20 medium dock leaves or 10 large leaves, with stems attached
- 500ml tomato passata
- 20g mint, finely chopped
- 100g feta, crumbled, to serve
- Pinch of salt

Dock leaves are often used as a wrapping leaf for dolma in Eastern Europe. The stem acts as a delicious tie to hold the filling within the leaves.

1. Cook the lentils and rice according to the packet instructions until tender, then drain and leave to cool.

2. Once cold, mix with the onion, raisins, sun-dried tomatoes, pistachios and herbs. Season with salt.

3. Preheat the oven to 150°C, 300°F, gas mark 2.

4. Boil a wide pan of water and plunge the dock leaves in for 30 seconds, then remove to a bowl of ice-cold water. Take out the leaves one at a time, shaking off any excess water, then lay them on a board and place a spoonful of the lentil and rice mix in the centre of the leaf. Roll the dock from the tip to the stem and use the stem to secure the dolma.

5. Place the dolmas into an ovenproof dish. Mix the passata and mint and pour over the dolmas. Cook for 30 minutes, then sprinkle the feta on top and serve with a leafy green salad.

DOCK STEM PECTIN

Makes 250ml pectin stock

- 500g dock stems
- Juice of 1 lemon

Pectin is a naturally occurring substance contained in the cell walls of plants and fruit. Pectin stock is an important tool in the armoury of the jam-maker to help make well-set jams. Dock stems are high in pectin and can easily be turned into a stock for making award-winning preserves.

1. Chop the dock stems into sticks that will fit into a cooking pan (do not use uncoated aluminium or copper pans, as the oxalic acid will react with the metal), pour in enough water to cover, as well as the lemon juice. Bring to the boil, cover the pan and turn down the heat to barely simmering, then cook until the stems have become so soft that they pull apart. (Check regularly to make sure that there is enough water in the pan and add more if required.) Once the stems have become mushy, turn off the heat and leave overnight.

2. The next day, strain the liquid through a muslin cloth into a pan, bring the liquid back to the boil and reduce by half. Pour into a sterilized bottle and pasteurize (see page 9) or store in the fridge for up to 1 week. If adding to low-pectin fruits when making jams, use roughly 150ml of stock per kilo of fruit.

DOCK LEAF, RICOTTA AND LEMON LINGUINE

Serves 4

- 500g fresh linguine or spaghetti
- 2 shallots or 1 white onion, finely sliced
- Butter or olive oil, for frying
- 100g dock leaves, finely sliced
- Zest and juice of ½ unwaxed lemon
- 150g ricotta
- Salt and freshly ground black pepper
- A few shavings of Parmesan

Finely shredded dock leaves are delicious served in cheese or cream sauces paired with chicken or griddled courgettes.

1. Cook the pasta in salted water according to the packet instructions, then drain and reserve one cup of the cooking water.

2. Return the pan to the heat and sweat the shallots in the butter or olive oil over a medium heat, until translucent and soft. Add the dock leaves and stir in the lemon zest, adding a ladle of pasta cooking water, and cook over a low heat until the dock leaves have softened, then add the lemon juice.

3. Stir the pasta into the pan and toss in the dock and lemon sauce. Stir in the ricotta and season with salt, pepper and Parmesan.

Caution: Avoid gathering mallow from inorganic nitrogen-rich soil, such as by roadsides, the plant could contain high levels of pollutants.

Mallow leaves have mid ribs that radiate clearly from the base of the leaf, dividing the leaves into five–seven sections or lobes. Leaves at the base of the plant tend to be more rounded; higher up the plant the leaves often become more deeply toothed. Leaves can be hairless or downy – some mallow species such as marshmallow have furry soft leaves. All mallow leaves are mild and nutty in flavour; use younger leaves in salads, older for cooking.

Mallow flowers have heart-shaped, pinkish-purple petals patterned with dark veins surrounding a cluster of long, fused-together stamens. The flowers are edible, fresh or dried.

Mallows can be sprawling plants, with numerous stems branching from a short central stem. They can grow up to 150cm high.

Mallow roots are rich in inulin and release a thick, soothing mucilage when they are cooked. Used in skincare and food, mucilage is renowned for healing and soothing.

Doughnut-shaped fruits grow from pollinated flowers containing crescent-shaped seeds. The young fruits can be eaten as a snack or pickled like capers.

Malva sylvestris

MALLOW

Malva spp.

DISTRIBUTION

Global, in both tropical and temperate regions.

HABITAT

Growing on most soil types, mallow thrives in uncultivated land, on wasteland (often urban) and by roadsides.

GATHERING SEASONS

Spring–autumn:
Young leaves to eat raw, older leaves to cook with.

Summer:
Flowers and fruits.

Autumn–early spring:
Roots.

The vast Malvaceae plant family ranges from large trees to common weeds, encompassing plants as diverse as cacao, durian, linden trees, hollyhock and the family's namesake, mallow.

Like many members of the same family, the individual plants can appear to have nothing in common, but one key tie is the significant amount of mucilage that many plants produce. Mucilage is contained in all plants; made up of long lengths of polysaccharide sugars, often held in seeds to help germination – soak chia or flaxseeds in water and the thick liquid that magically appears is its store of mucilage being released. Plants also have some levels of mucilage in their roots, forming a two-way bridge between the soil and plants that helps plants absorb nutrients, and feeds bacteria and fungi in the soil in a symbiotic relationship. The mucilage in roots leaches a range of organic molecules into the soil, including the very building blocks of life – enzymes, proteins, DNA, sugars and amino acids.

Most plants in the Malvaceae family are crammed full of the slippery stuff and the mucilage in mallow is why we eat marshmallow sweets, why you will often find mallow extract in skincare products, but also why we rarely eat the plant. Mucilage, its greatest asset, is to many off-putting, which is a great shame, as mallow contains blood-sugar-controlling inulin, antioxidant-rich phenols, and vitamins A, B and C as well as the soothing mucilage, healing and nourishing and soothing our skin, airways and gut membranes. Used for thousands of years as food and medicine, mallow is never far from human habitation, thriving on disturbed nitrogen-rich soil that grows wherever we set up camp, or even vast cities; rural and urban foragers do not need to venture far to find mallow and its incredible mucilage, quietly going about its business like all plants, keeping the earth alive.

MALLOW

The benefits and abundance of mallow make its slippery texture worth learning to love, just as it is in Middle Eastern countries, where it is often blended with other, firmer textures and ingredients.

Young emerging leaves are tender enough to be added raw along with the flowers to salads. The older leaves can be fried as crisps or used as a vegetable, added to soups such as the Middle Eastern *molokhia*, as wrapping leaves in dolmas, wilted with onions and garlic, or chopped finely and added to bean burgers, falafels or cheese-filled filo pies. Flowers are sweetly nutty in flavour and can be used in both sweet and savoury dishes.

MALLOW ROOT AND HONEY HALVA
Makes about 20 portions

- 500ml honey
- 2 tbsp ground mallow root (or 30g fresh root, finely grated)
- 350g tahini paste
- 200g shelled unsalted pistachio nuts, roughly chopped (optional)

The ancient Egyptians were the first people who wrote about using mallow – the marshes of the Nile were home to swathes of marshmallow, and the plant was used in a forerunner of halva, with honey and nuts, as an ambrosial relief from coughs for nobility, Pharaohs and gods. Fortunately, times change, and it is now perfectly fine to eat this ancient Egyptian-inspired sweet treat, even if you are not a god with a cough.

1. Place the honey in a heavy-based pan and add the mallow root, then place over a low heat for 30 minutes to allow the flavour of the mallow to infuse into the honey. Strain the mallow and put the honey back in the pan, and heat to 115°C on a sugar thermometer.

2. Warm the tahini paste in another pan, and when warmed through, stir the infused honey into the paste for 5 minutes. Add chopped nuts, if desired, and pour into an oiled dish. Refrigerate for up to 36 hours before slicing into blocks and serving.

MALLOW ROOT MARSHMALLOWS
Makes 20 squares

- 1 tbsp ground mallow root or 10cm fresh root
- 500ml just-boiled water
- 125g sugar
- 75g glucose syrup
- 1 egg white
- 1 tsp vanilla extract, orange blossom water or rose water
- Ground nuts, cornflour and icing sugar, for dusting

Ever since mallow was infused with honey in ancient Egypt, it was eaten as a sweet treat, often for its medicinal benefits. It took a jump of a few thousand years to France in 1800s for marshmallow sweets to be created; infusing mallow in sugar created *pâte de guimauve*, a medicinal confectionery. Eventually mallow roots were replaced with gelatine, heralding today's fluffy confection, no longer with the delicious benefits brought by its namesake.

1. Add the ground mallow root or fresh root to the just-boiled water in a pan. Leave on a low heat, stirring occasionally, until the liquid thickens. Strain and pour 100ml of the liquid into a saucepan with the sugar and glucose syrup. Bring the mixture to a rapid boil until it reaches 121°C on a sugar thermometer.

2. In a bowl, whisk the egg white until it forms stiff peaks, and with the whisk still running, slowly pour in the mallow-root-infused sugar syrup. Keep whisking for up to 10 minutes until the mixture is whipped. Add the vanilla, orange blossom or rose water, pour into an oiled dish and leave to set overnight. Cut into cubes and dust with ground nuts, cornflour and icing sugar.

MALLOW FALAFELS
Serves 4

- 125g dried fava (broad) beans or chickpeas, soaked overnight
- 1 onion, grated
- 125g mallow leaves, thoroughly washed and dried
- 1 garlic clove
- ½ tsp ground cumin
- ½ tsp ground coriander
- 20g mint leaves
- 1 tbsp flour (wheat flour or chickpea flour)
- ½ tsp salt
- Vegetable oil, for frying (optional)

The origins of falafel are claimed by many Middle Eastern countries; Egyptian falafels are made with fava beans, Israeli often with chickpeas. Wherever the balls originated from, and whichever pulses are used, they are all delicious blended with mallow.

1. Rinse the soaked pulses, place all of the ingredients apart from the oil into a food processor and blend until the pulses resemble slightly sticky couscous. Put the mixture in a bowl, stir it all together, taking out any large pieces of bean or chickpea, and place in a fridge to settle. After an hour, remove from the fridge, roll into walnut-sized balls and either bake in an oven at 180°C, 350°F, gas mark 4 for 20 minutes or shallow-fry until golden brown.

2. Serve with salads and dunk into Middle Eastern-inspired dips.

YARROW

Achillea millefolium

● DISTRIBUTION

Native to Asia, Europe and
North America, introduced
to South America, New
Zealand and Australia.

● HABITAT

Grasslands, gardens, verges, in
dry, damp, stony and loamy
soils.

**● GATHERING
SEASONS**

Mid-spring–autumn:
Young feathery basal leaves.

Summer–early autumn:
Flowers and leaves.

A diminutive perennial with a big aromatic flavour, yarrow grows
inconspicuously yet often abundantly in established grassland – both
wild and domesticated. Feathery leaves grow straight from the ground
in the spring, followed by umbels of beautiful white and sometimes
pink-tinged flowers, on long, furry stems, making it easier to spot
amongst longer grasses than when it's in leaf alone.

It may hide amongst the grass, but it has over 120 useful compounds
held in its feathery leaves and has been sought out for thousands of
years for its medicinal value. Recently in Spain a 50,000-year-old
human skull was found to have traces of yarrow and chamomile
ground into its teeth; yarrow is extremely bitter when chewed and
the early human would probably have been eating it as a medicinal
plant, grazing on it in much the same way that animals instinctively
search out and graze on beneficial plants in their environments today.

The catalogue of traditional uses for yarrow is long and impressive.
Yarrow has been used to treat a great number of ailments, ranging
from soothing toothache to healing wounds, calming anxiety and
regulating periods, to pain relief. Perhaps the ancient human had
toothache? Whether they were searching out a cure or simply
enjoying the flavour of the plant, yarrow's culinary use is firmly
within the bounds of flavouring. Yarrow contains small amounts of
a compound called thujone; although this is also found in plants
such as sage and tarragon, it is inadvisable to eat in large quantities.
Fortunately yarrow's perfumed, bitter flavour mean a small amount is
all that is needed to add a delicious flavour to seasonings and food.

Growing at the top of the stem, large, closely packed clusters of tiny 'florets' (individual flowers) with petals that range from creamy white to dusty pink. The flowers can be used in bitter herbal infusions.

In Spain yarrow is called *plumajillo*, meaning 'little feather'. Its feathery, fern-like leaves grow directly from the ground and around the flowering stem, which is tender with a mildly bitter flavour when young, becoming stronger in flavour as it ages.

Growing from 30cm to 1 metre tall in uncut grasslands, the tough flowering stems have a white, fine fluffy covering.

YARROW

Yarrow leaves have a long history of flavouring food and drink as well as being used in traditional medicine. Historically the most widespread use was to flavour and preserve beer. Ginger and yarrow blend together harmoniously, as do many other ingredients with yarrow; it is bitter enough to play a key role in vermouths but aromatic enough to be infused in oils, syrups and salts. As a fresh herb, it is at home alongside other Mediterranean aromatics and ingredients and can be added to seasonings such as za'atar.

YARROW, GINGER AND ELDERFLOWER CORDIAL
Makes 1 litre

- 600g sugar
- 10 elderflower heads, with yellow-tinged pollen on
- 100g yarrow stems, leaves and flowers
- 25g fresh root ginger, coarsely grated
- 1 organic lemon, thinly sliced
- 1 tsp citric acid (or an extra lemon if preferred)

The combination of yarrow and elderflower is often used by herbalists to ease symptoms of winter colds. Ginger adds another weapon in the virus-fighting armoury, and happens to pair deliciously with both yarrow and elderflower. Yarrow extract is in fact frequently used in ginger beer to provide an antibacterial preserving agent, improving the flavour at the same time.

This cordial is delicious drunk on hot summer days in soft drinks or cocktails, but make enough to see you through the winter months as well.

1. Bring 600ml water to the boil in a pan, add the sugar and heat, stirring, until dissolved. Leave to cool for 10 minutes. Add the elderflowers, yarrow, ginger and lemon to the syrup. Add the citric acid, if using. Cover and leave overnight.

2. Warm the syrup and pour through a fine muslin cloth-lined sieve. Pour into sterilized bottles and store in the fridge or freezer (leaving at least 10 per cent of the bottle empty if storing in the freezer to allow for expansion).

YARROW AND TOMATO SALAD

Serves 4

- 8 large ripe tomatoes, at room temperature
- A few sprigs of yarrow stem with leaves and flowers
- 2 shallots or a handful of onion greens, finely chopped
- Olive oil, for drizzling
- Salt

Yarrow is sensational used instead of, or paired with, basil, and just like basil, yarrow's aromatic, bitter flavour is perfect for seasoning summer food, such as this most simple but mouth-watering of tomato salads.

1. Thinly slice the tomatoes from top to bottom, and lay on a serving plate. Pull the yarrow leaves and flowers into small pieces (about ½cm). Evenly scatter the yarrow and shallot or onion greens across the tomatoes, drizzle with olive oil and a sprinkle of salt and serve at room temperature with bread or as a side salad.

YARROW, MARJORAM AND CHIVE FLOWER SALT

Makes 120g

- 30g yarrow leaves and tender stems
- 30g fresh wild marjoram or oregano
- 30g chive flowers or spring onions
- 30g sea salt flakes

Yarrow and wild marjoram are often found growing in the same poor sun-baked soil, two perfumed herbs that both have intense but complementary flavours. With the addition of chives, yarrow and marjoram turn into an incredibly delicious savoury salt, that can be used to season meats, breads, vegetables, grains and even to lend an umami flavour to martinis.

1. Roughly chop the yarrow leaves and stems, pull off the leaves from the marjoram or oregano and half of the chive flowers or spring onions. Place in a spice grinder with the salt and grind until fine – the salt will be slightly claggy at this point. Stir in the remaining chive flowers (picked off the main flower head) and spread the salt mixture on a flat plate. Place in sunlight or in a warm, dry place to dry out for a few hours.

2. Store in an airtight jar and serve with everything.

MEADOWSWEET

Filipendula ulmaria

As elderflower and wild roses disappear from hedgerows, it is the turn of ditches to be adorned with scented blooms and meadowsweet; the Queen of the Ditch is in every way as beautiful as the flowers it replaces. Lining rural roads and marshy fields with clouds of cream flowers, the warm summer air becomes filled with its sweet vanilla and almond fragrance, and when the flowers are dried, they release the iconic scent of a warm summer day – that of drying hay meadows. Like the grasses and clover in hay, meadowsweet contains coumarin – a chemical produced by plants as a natural pesticide, which becomes stronger smelling when dried. Coumarin is repellent to pests but seductive to people; dried meadowsweet was historically strewn on floors and scattered at weddings to sweeten the path of brides, leading to the use of modern-day confetti.

But the alluring flower wasn't exclusively used as an air freshener, it was often added to food and drink; meadowsweet was an original ingredient in Nordic mead, a delicious brew made with honey. The Nordic brewers may have added meadowsweet because of its sweet scent, or they may have been more astute in their addition, because alongside the hay flavour of coumarin, meadowsweet leaves and stems have an antiseptic ointment aroma, this time coming from salicylates, which were extracted from meadowsweet in the nineteenth century to develop aspirin. Meadowsweet has long been used as a herbal painkiller, soothing sore heads, stomachs and aching joints. Perhaps it is time to reintroduce meadowsweet to wedding parties, but this time in hangover-curing champagnes and meads, rather than scattered on the floor.

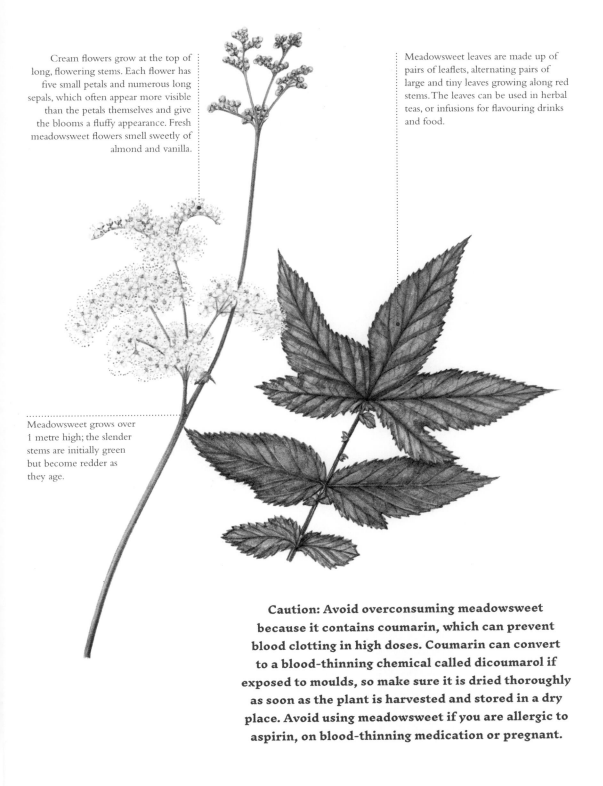

Cream flowers grow at the top of long, flowering stems. Each flower has five small petals and numerous long sepals, which often appear more visible than the petals themselves and give the blooms a fluffy appearance. Fresh meadowsweet flowers smell sweetly of almond and vanilla.

Meadowsweet leaves are made up of pairs of leaflets, alternating pairs of large and tiny leaves growing along red stems. The leaves can be used in herbal teas, or infusions for flavouring drinks and food.

Meadowsweet grows over 1 metre high; the slender stems are initially green but become redder as they age.

Caution: Avoid overconsuming meadowsweet because it contains coumarin, which can prevent blood clotting in high doses. Coumarin can convert to a blood-thinning chemical called dicoumarol if exposed to moulds, so make sure it is dried thoroughly as soon as the plant is harvested and stored in a dry place. Avoid using meadowsweet if you are allergic to aspirin, on blood-thinning medication or pregnant.

MEADOWSWEET

Fresh meadowsweet flowers are often used in sweet dishes; best infused at low temperatures into syrups and creams. The scent is subtle but the flavour is strong, so a little goes a long way and a couple of teaspoons of flowers will flavour a litre of liquid – dairy, nut milk or syrup. Meadowsweet can be used to create panna cottas, ice creams and nougats.

MEADOWSWEET MEAD
Makes 5 litres

- 600ml raw honey
- 4½ litres unchlorinated water
- 4–5 organic raisins
- 4 organic grapes or 2 plums
- A handful of freshly picked or thoroughly dried meadowsweet flowers and clover flowers (fresh flowers will give a different flavour to dried)
- 1 tsp lemon juice

You will need:
- 5-litre food-grade pail or bowl
- 2 demijohns
- Sterilized wooden stick or long-handled spoon

Mead is a simple fermented drink made by diluting honey in water. Traditional meads were flavoured with meadowsweet; this recipe includes clover in a nod to the shared coumarin. If you favour a quicker, less alcoholic fermentation, follow an elderflower champagne recipe, replacing elderflowers with meadowsweet.

1. Heat the honey and water together in a large pan until the honey has dissolved. Pour into the container, add the raisins, fruit, flowers and lemon juice, cover with a cloth and place in a warm, dark place. Keep the stick in the liquid, but make sure the top protrudes above the water so that you don't contaminate the mead when you stir it. Stir the liquid well three times each day.

2. After 5–10 days the liquid will become foamy and start fermenting. Pour into a demijohn, seal with an airlock and leave in a dark place for four weeks. Then siphon the liquid into another demijohn, leaving behind the sediment. Leave for up to six months, when the mead is ready to bottle and drink.

MEADOWSWEET MIDWINTER BUNS – LUSSEBULLAR

Makes 12

- 250ml milk
- 10g dried meadowsweet leaves and flowers
- 75g salted butter
- 450g bread flour
- 1 tsp baking powder
- 75g sugar
- 7g fast-action dried yeast
- 1 egg, beaten
- 20g icing sugar

In Norway, Sweden and Finland, St Lucia's Day – the original shortest day of the year – is celebrated with Lussebullar buns. We've replaced the traditional saffron flavouring in these sweet buns with dried meadowsweet to evoke the warmer days to come.

1. Heat the milk in a pan over a low heat until warm; infuse 5g of the meadowsweet in the milk over the heat for 30 minutes, then take off the heat and strain out the flowers.

2. Melt the butter in another pan and stir into the milk. Mix together the flour, baking powder, sugar and yeast in a bowl, stir in the milk mixture and form a dough. Knead for 5–10 minutes, cover and leave to prove until doubled in size.

3. Once proved, knead again for a few seconds and divide into 12 equal pieces. Roll into lengths, and curl into S shapes; place on baking sheets and prove for another 30 minutes.

4. Preheat the oven to 220°C, 425°F, gas mark 7. Brush the rolls with beaten egg and bake in the oven for 8–10 minutes or until golden. Serve dusted in icing sugar mixed with the remaining meadowsweet.

MEADOWSWEET ELIXIR

Makes 500ml

- 100g fresh meadowsweet
- 400ml vodka
- 100ml glycerine

Like many plants that are both medicinal and edible, infusions made with meadowsweet can often jump from herbalists' apothecaries onto cocktail makers' shelves. Traditionally used to soothe aches and pains, meadowsweet elixir has a bitter, tannic but floral flavour; and is delicious dropped into martinis or sour cherry cocktails. To capture just the sweet scent of meadowsweet in vodka, infuse the flowers for only a few hours before straining.

1. Place all the ingredients in a jar, press a weight onto the flowers to ensure they stay in the liquid, seal and macerate for 4–6 weeks. Strain through a muslin cloth, bottle and label. Take ½ to 1 teaspoon when required – preferably in a medicinal cocktail.

Large, classically daisy-like flowers growing up to 5cm wide. As with other members of the daisy family, each flower is actually a composite; composed of numerous individual flowers or florets – yellow disk florets in the centre and white ray florets around the edge. They are designed to make the plant as attractive and visible as possible to pollinators, a strategy that works well, with up to 20,000 seeds able to be produced on vigorous plants. Oxeye daisy flowers have a chamomile taste and can be used in teas, syrups and oils in its place.

Flat, unopened flower buds perch at the end of each stem, full of perfume and bite. Gather them in the early summer to pickle or add to salads.

Oxeye daisy plants can grow up to 80cm high. The branched, rigid stems are downy towards the base of the plant, getting less hairy higher up the stem. The stems, when tender, can be added to salads, but later, when still full of flavour, can be ground into salts for seasoning.

The toothed leaves growing at the base of the plant have a distinctive spoon shape, making them ideal carriers for canapés. The aromatic, slightly peppery leaves are delicious in salads. Growing up to 10cm in length, they become smaller, slimmer and more toothed as they grow up the stem.

OXEYE DAISY

Leucanthemum vulgare

❧ DISTRIBUTION

Native to Europe and Asia, introduced and invasive in America, Australia and New Zealand.

❧ HABITAT

Meadows and fields, verges and grassy scrubland.

❧ GATHERING SEASONS

Early spring:
Young basal leaves.

Mid-spring:
Tender flowering stems.

Late spring–early summer:
Unopened flowers.

Summer:
Opened flowers, leaves, stems.

Knee-high wispy daisy flowers signal the end of spring and the beginning of summer on road verges, in fields and meadows. A beautiful but problematic plant to farmers, oxeye daisy charms its way into food crops and grazing meadows. Its distinctive perfumed taste is delicious to people but unappealing to livestock, so it grows unabated, crowding out crops and dominating the flavour of hay meadows. In Scotland, oxeye daisy contaminated fields of monoculture crops so much that farmers were historically forced to pay additional taxes if they had the flowers opening on their land. When introduced to America in the 1800s, the giant daisies swiftly spread through prairie and grazing land fast enough to be categorized as a noxious invasive plant. The good news for people is that its invasive tendencies make it a prime plant for us to gather – learn to identify the peppery, lemony, aromatic plant and you can become the grazer who keeps the plant under control.

All above-ground parts of the oxeye daisy are edible. Each spring oxeye daisy, a long-lived perennial, emerges from the ground with rosettes of spoon-shaped, frilled succulent leaves. By late spring tight button-like flower buds have grown on long stems, lined with smaller, thinner leaves growing from the stem. As the days lengthen and warm, so oxeye daisy opens, its large swaying flowers almost glowing in the late evening dusk of the summer. You may know oxeye daisy as moon daisy – its romantic name gained from the glow of many mini moons radiating from invaded meadows on long midsummer evenings.

OXEYE DAISY

Oxeye daisy's lemon and aromatic flavours make it a plant that can dance between sweet and savoury food, drinks and seasonings. Its succulent texture makes it ideal for preserving and eating in salads. Oxeye is in the same family of plants as chrysanthemums; plants which are widely used in East Asian cookery, and it can be used in place of edible chrysanthemums in many recipes. Flash-fry or swiftly steam the leaves and tender stems. Long contact with heat destroys the flavour, so treat it with a swift hand and minimal cooking. Tougher older stems are still full of flavour and can be ground into salts and sugars, which can be used as seasonings to flavour salads, grains, fish and meat or cocktails and granitas.

OXEYE DAISY SALAD
Serves 4 as a side salad

- 150g rocket leaves
- 25g finely torn chicory or dandelion leaves
- 50g oxeye daisy leaves
- Lemon juice and olive oil, or your favourite vinaigrette

The young fleshy leaves of oxeye daisy are perfumed and peppery. Victorian writer John Claudius Loudon spoke of Italian salads of chicory, rocket and oxeye daisy leaves – the blend of bitter, perfumed and peppery make this a sensational pairing in a fresh salad which appeals to all the senses. The pepperiness heightens the sour lemon flavour in the daisy and the bitter taste of chicory brings out its sweetness – a simple but perfectly balanced piece of Italian flavour pairing.

1. Wash and dry the leaves, dress with either lemon juice and oil or a favourite vinaigrette.

SALTED OXEYE DAISY FLOWER BUD CAPERS
Makes a 150g jar

- 50g fresh, tightly closed oxeye daisy flower buds
- ½ tsp sea salt
- ½ tsp Sichuan peppercorns
- 125ml white wine vinegar or cider vinegar

Capered oxeye daisy flower buds are offered for sale in northern American states and Canada, harvested from the abundant fields of flowers, and can be served in the same way as capers. The leaves and buds of both oxeye daisy and Sichuan peppercorns cause a tingling sensation in your mouth, and a few peppercorns added to the vinegar heighten this tingly treat.

1. Wash the oxeye daisy buds and dry thoroughly. Pack the buds into a preserving jar with the salt and peppercorns. Bring the vinegar to the boil and pour over the buds, filling the jar to the rim. Secure with sterilized lids, and store in a cool, dark cupboard to mature for a couple of weeks before eating.

CORIANDER AND OXEYE DAISY FRESH CHUTNEY
Makes 100g

- 25g oxeye daisy leaves
- 15g fresh coriander leaves
- 2 tbsp lime juice
- 1 green chilli, halved and deseeded
- ½ garlic clove, crushed
- 1 tbsp natural yoghurt
- ½ tsp sugar
- ¼ cucumber, coarsely grated
- Salt and freshly ground black pepper

Oxeye daisy is at home paired with coriander; the perfumed flavours of each plant complement each other excellently. This fiery, fresh chutney is delicious served as a sauce, dip or marinade.

1. Blend the oxeye daisy and coriander leaves with lime juice, chilli, garlic and yoghurt to a rough purée, and season with sugar, salt and pepper. Squeeze out excess liquid from the grated cucumber and stir into the puréed mixture. Refrigerate for at least an hour before serving, to allow the flavours to develop.

2. Delicious served with curries or as a dip. Flavours such as lemongrass, Thai basil and Sichuan peppercorns work well in this recipe, too.

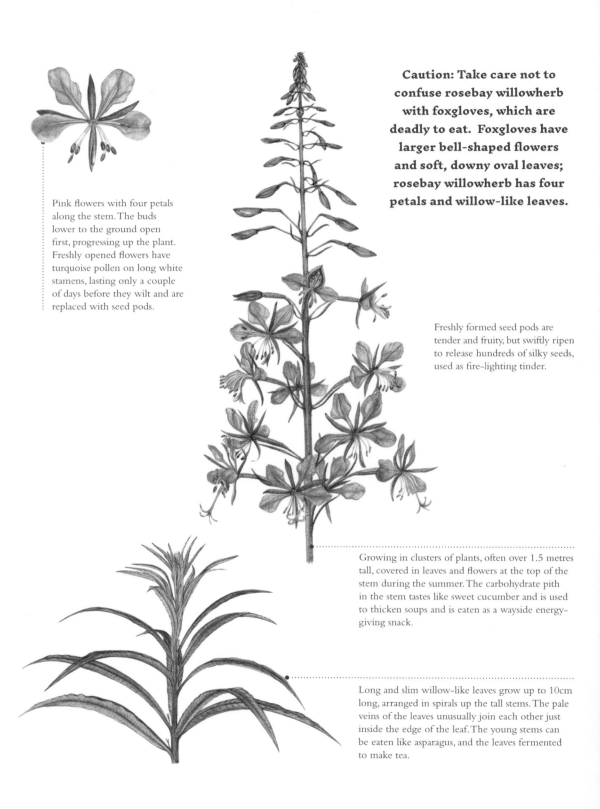

Pink flowers with four petals along the stem. The buds lower to the ground open first, progressing up the plant. Freshly opened flowers have turquoise pollen on long white stamens, lasting only a couple of days before they wilt and are replaced with seed pods.

Caution: Take care not to confuse rosebay willowherb with foxgloves, which are deadly to eat. Foxgloves have larger bell-shaped flowers and soft, downy oval leaves; rosebay willowherb has four petals and willow-like leaves.

Freshly formed seed pods are tender and fruity, but swiftly ripen to release hundreds of silky seeds, used as fire-lighting tinder.

Growing in clusters of plants, often over 1.5 metres tall, covered in leaves and flowers at the top of the stem during the summer. The carbohydrate pith in the stem tastes like sweet cucumber and is used to thicken soups and is eaten as a wayside energy-giving snack.

Long and slim willow-like leaves grow up to 10cm long, arranged in spirals up the tall stems. The pale veins of the leaves unusually join each other just inside the edge of the leaf. The young stems can be eaten like asparagus, and the leaves fermented to make tea.

ROSEBAY WILLOWHERB

Chamaenerion angustifolium

◈ DISTRIBUTION

Native to Alaska and Siberia,
now almost global.

◈ HABITAT

Well-drained ground; thrives
on wasteland, forest clearings
and disturbed ground.

**◈ GATHERING
SEASONS**

Autumn–spring:
Roots.

Spring:
Young emerging shoots.

Summer:
Pith inside stems, flowers and
freshly forming seed pods.

The tall, pink, wafting spires of rosebay willowherb flower in late summer and can turn bare land into a sea of colour; teeming with pollinators, their legs covered with the flowers' pale turquoise pollen. Where all seems dead, rosebay willowherb brings life – one of the remarkable pioneer plants, rosebay willowherb thrives in scorched earth, forest clearings and even bomb sites, turning desolation into swathes of pink.

Rosebay willowherb's origins are thought to reside in Siberia, and just as people slowly spread over the Bering land mass that was exposed by the last Ice Age, eventually settling in Alaska and spreading across the Americas, so rosebay willowherb's seeds and roots took advantage of the lower sea levels and spread into Alaska. Once in America, just like in Siberia, the plant not only provided food and medicine but also improved the soil of the tundra, paving the way for other species to thrive and nourish the new human population.

Like the early American envoys who would have searched for new habitats, fluffy rosebay willowherb seeds can be seen wafting across urban and rural landscapes, looking for niches in which to establish themselves to set up new colonies of the plant. Once established, most rosebay willowherbs stay close to their home roots, growing in clusters that can survive for over 35 years, from suckers attached to the original plant, until adventurous seeds come of age and travel to new lands.

ROSEBAY WILLOWHERB

For thousands of years, rosebay willowherb has been used as a medicine thanks to its soothing, anti-inflammatory properties. Rich in vitamin C, all parts of rosebay willowherb are edible with an acidic, slightly astringent flavour. The carbohydrate-rich roots can be eaten as a vegetable, young shoots steamed like asparagus, leaves fermented into teas, and the tart, fruity tasting flowers used in jellies, syrups and vinegars.

ROSEBAY WILLOWHERB LEAF TEA (KOPORYE)

Makes 1 jar

- 300g willowherb leaves

Fermented rosebay willowherb leaves make a fruity, dark tea. Made in Russia since the twelfth century, it was at one point widely exported across Europe and drunk as commonly as other teas. Quite why rosebay willowherb tea lost its popularity outside of Russia is disputed. Some say the Russian Revolution resulted in the collapse of production, others claim the East India Company launched a smear campaign against the tea, discrediting and wiping out the competition it posed to Indian brews. Crammed full of flavonoids, iron, copper, calcium and vitamin C, anti-inflammatory, astringent and antimicrobial, rosebay willowherb tea was a worthy competitor – victim perhaps to age-old fake news.

1. To make rosebay willowherb tea, gather leaves when the plant is about to (or already in) flower. Run your hands down the stalk to gather handfuls at a time, leaving the flowers and buds above. Place the leaves in a tray or basket overnight, when they will start to wilt.

2. The next day, roll bundles of the leaves in your hands until they have softened. Place them in a glass jar for two or three days, checking every day, as they will soon start to release a fruity aroma.

3. At this point, dry the leaves in a low oven (50°C) until they have dried completely. Seal in airtight containers. Make your tea by pouring just-boiled water over a teaspoon of leaves. Leave to steep for 5 to 10 minutes before enjoying the fruity brew whilst reading a piece of made-up news.

ROSEBAY WILLOWHERB SHOOT REFRIGERATOR PICKLES

Makes 300g

....

- 250ml white wine vinegar or apple cider vinegar
- 1 tbsp sea salt
- 50g sugar
- 1 medium onion, sliced
- 1 tsp mustard seeds
- 1 tsp dill seeds
- 1 tsp dried chilli flakes
- 1 tsp black peppercorns
- 3 spruce/pine tips (if you have access to them)
- 100g rosebay willowherb shoots, washed and dried

....

Rosebay willowherb shoots grow in the spring; the sweet, delicious young shoots become more strongly flavoured as they age. In Alaska the plant, known as *ciilaaq*, grows abundantly in the tundra. The benefits of eating rosebay willowherb are promoted by the forward-thinking Alaskan government as a sustainable superfood, one that helps lower cholesterol, protecting against diabetes and other diseases. This recipe is an instant pickle, to be eaten the day after making. If you want to preserve your shoots for longer, use a recipe for lacto-fermenting vegetables (see page 190).

1. To make the pickling brine, mix together 250ml of water with the vinegar, salt and sugar and bring to a boil until the sugar and salt have dissolved. Take off the heat and cool to room temperature.

2. Place the onion, spices, spruce tips and the rosebay willowherb shoots tightly into a preserving jar with a vinegar-proof lid. Pour the brine over the shoots and keep topping up until any air bubbles have dispersed and the jar is full of brine. Seal and store in a refrigerator for up to 2 weeks.

ROSEBAY WILLOWHERB SYRUP

Makes around 500ml

....

- 1-litre container of rosebay willowherb flowers
- 500g sugar
- 3 tbsp lemon juice

....

Rosebay willowherb flowers have an astringent, fruity, almost bitter flavour, a lot like cranberries and, just like cranberries, are incredible made into jelly condiments using either apple, redcurrant or dock stem (see Dock stem pectin recipe, page 131) as pectin bases. They also make a fantastically tart and sweet syrup that can be added to cocktails or turned into sorbets.

1. Pour 300ml just-boiled water over the flowers in a wide-necked jar, pushing the flowers under the water, and cover for 30 minutes or until the flowers lose their colour to the water.

2. In a heavy-based pan, heat 200ml water and add the sugar, then simmer, stirring, until the sugar has dissolved. Cool for 10 minutes. Strain the flower water into the sugar syrup, stir, and add the lemon juice; the acid in the lemon juice will turn the syrup a deep magenta, like the flowers' original colour.

3. Store in sterilized bottles and pasteurize (see page 9) or keep in the fridge until a fruity flower syrup is required.

WILD STRAWBERRY

Fragaria vesca

🔖 **DISTRIBUTION**

Different species of wild strawberry grow globally.

🔖 **HABITAT**

Clearings, embankments, farmland, woodland margins and gardens. Often hidden in long grasses.

🔖 **GATHERING SEASONS**

Spring–summer:
Young tender leaves for teas and salads.

Early summer–early autumn:
Fruit.

During cold months supporters of locally grown food ignore strawberries flown in from warmer lands, patiently waiting until low-food-mile fruit fill the aisles and stalls; punnets of long-awaited plump fruit which are often more impressive in size than taste. Locally grown strawberries may tick all the right seasonal-eating boxes, but the strawberries we have available today were only made possible due to the global import and export of wild strawberries 300 years ago.

All across the world different species of wild strawberries grow, hugging woodland floors, grassland and even beaches. The deeply flavoured fruit have been eaten for thousands of years, but for hundreds of those our human urge to make things bigger and better led to countless attempts to cross-breed the different petite plants to create the perfect-flavoured large fruit. Wild strawberries were taken to and brought back from colonized lands to be cross-bred, with some success. But still the berry was small, and our appetite for something larger was unabated.

Only in 1704, when a French spy, aptly named Amédée Frézier (derived from *fraise*, French for strawberry), was assigned to Chile to investigate the Spanish colonists' defence and farming practices, was the parent of all large strawberries discovered. Monsieur Frézier was overwhelmed when he saw fields of huge native strawberries growing successfully. Laden with plants and defence plans, he returned to France, where the plant grew, spreading suckers but no fruit until a chance cross-breeding with another import – a more flavoursome, small North American plant brought back by European settlers. The offspring was large but not as delicious as wild strawberries. However, big strawberries are easier to harvest than the tiny wild crop, which soon fell out of favour, being relegated to woodlands, grassy verges and under hedgerows. But as anyone who has tasted a ripe wild strawberry on a summer's day knows, wildly seasonal and wildly local tastes are far better than the imports.

Growing with sets of three leaflets at the end of hairy stems, the small toothed leaves have a mildly fruity herbal flavour. Young leaves can be eaten raw, older ones added to infusions and tea.

Small, five-petalled white flowers measure up to 2cm across. Flowers start forming in mid-spring, when surrounding grasses haven't hidden the plant from view. Remember where you found the flowers, then in the summer, look around the base of long grasses and you'll find the hidden fruit.

Little red juicy berries, covered with pinhead-sized fruits which look like seeds. Wild strawberries are intense in flavour, containing immune-boosting ellagic acid.

WILD STRAWBERRY

What wild strawberries lack in stature they make up for in taste;
delicious simply scattered on salads, summer cakes and ice creams.
Preserving makes the most of wild strawberries' intense flavour,
making delicious liqueurs, jams and sauces either in sugar, alcohol or
vinegar. Fresh young leaves are slightly astringent and mildly herbal,
perfect added to a spring or summer mixed leaf salad. Traditionally
turned into herbal teas, the leaves are rich in tannins and antioxidants,
with a taste not far from green tea. Either use fresh or thoroughly
dried leaves (do not use wilted leaves as they can develop toxicity).

WILD STRAWBERRIES PRESERVED IN SYRUP
Makes a 300g jar

- 100g wild strawberries
- 150g sugar
- 400g cultivated strawberries
- Pinch of citric acid (optional)

Preserving wild strawberries in syrup
is a delicious way to capture their
flavour. This recipe makes use of their
cultivated cousins with a strawberry
syrup to suspend the little wild
berries in.

1. Place the wild strawberries in
a bowl, toss with some of the
sugar and leave overnight in the
fridge to macerate (this will help
the strawberries stay firm).

2. The following day, preheat the
oven to 170°C, 325°F, gas mark 3.
Place the cultivated strawberries
in an ovenproof dish, cover with
baking paper and bake for 20–30
minutes or until the strawberries
are soft and the dish full of juices.
Strain the juices and pour into a pan
with the remaining sugar, and heat,
stirring, until the sugar has dissolved.
(The remaining cooked strawberries
need not be wasted – use them as a
delicious compote). Add any syrupy
juices that have come out of the wild
strawberries, then gently simmer
until the syrup starts to thicken –
taste the syrup, if it is too sweet, add
a pinch of citric acid. Stir the wild
strawberries into the syrup, place in
jars and seal while hot. This will keep
for a couple of weeks in the fridge,
or longer if pasteurized (see page 9).

WILD STRAWBERRIES AND CREAM SEMIFREDDO

Serves 4

- 3 large egg yolks, plus 1 large egg
- 70g sugar
- 400ml double cream
- 50g wild strawberries

WILD STRAWBERRY GRAPPA

Makes 500ml

- 150g wild strawberries
- Zest of ½ lemon
- 75g sugar
- 500ml grappa

Strawberries and cream were first served using wild strawberries at lavish Tudor banquets at Hampton Court in England. After elaborate, multi-course feasts were served to hundreds of guests, the chef who suggested serving strawberries with cream must have been a hero to exhausted kitchen staff. Almost as easy to make is a semifreddo, which the savvy chef probably would have served if he had a freezer handy.

1. Make a bain-marie by heating 3cm of water in a pan and selecting a heatproof bowl that fits on top. Before putting it over the pan, whisk the egg yolks, egg and sugar in the bowl. When they are whisked and pale yellow, place the bowl over the saucepan, whisking continuously until the mixture thickens. Remove from the heat and place in a second bowl of cold water to cool.

2. While the mixture is cooling, whisk the cream to stiff peaks in another bowl. Gently fold the cream and strawberries into the mixture. Pour into a small pan lined with cling film and place in the freezer until frozen. Serve at regal feasts.

A few handfuls of wild strawberries can be eaten in a moment or turned into a bottle of flavour that can be dripped onto dozens of dishes, or sipped straight as a liqueur. In northern Italy, grappa distilleries sit at the foot of hills decorated with wild strawberries. Grappa and strawberries are used to create this special drink, but it would work as well with vodka or aquavit. Whichever base is used, the key to the liqueur's success lies in macerating the fruit before adding the alcohol.

1. Push the fruit and lemon zest into a bottle, cover with sugar and place in a sunny place for a month or until the strawberries have released all of their juice into the sugar.

2. Add the grappa and leave for another couple of months before filtering, then store for another two months before drinking. By the time the drink is ready it will be nearly Christmas – the perfect excuse to drink it mixed with sparkling wine.

HORSERADISH

Armoracia rusticana

❧ DISTRIBUTION

Native to southeast
Europe and West Asia, now
naturalized and cultivated in
most temperate regions of
the world.

❧ HABITAT

Full sun and partial shade.
Horseradish spreads by its
roots; you can often find long
colonies of it alongside roads.

**❧ GATHERING
SEASONS**

Autumn–spring:
Roots.

Spring–late summer:
Leaves.

Identified by clumps of donkey-ear-like leaves, horseradish is better known for its thick, pungent roots that spread in a galloping fashion through the ground, forming large clumps of leaves that grow up to 1 metre in height. Horseradish has been used since ancient times for its potent flavour and medicinal properties. Crammed full of mustard oils, this fiery member of the mustard family jostles with wasabi for king of mustard-kick status. Horseradish proliferates by spreading its roots, escaping from old vegetable gardens and travelling across fields until it hits a roadway and can't spread onwards, sending its roots out along the side of the road. Many countries have legislation about uprooting wild plants, and you cannot go along with a spade and dig up horseradish root on public verges, but the leaves are legitimate gathering and contain large amounts of the compounds that gives horseradish its distinctive nasal-clearing punch.

Horseradish is thought to originate from Slavic Eastern Europe, where it has been used since antiquity. Known as *khren*, both the leaves and roots are still used in a wide range of dishes today. Ancient Greeks and Romans followed the Slavs' lead, but not using the root as food, rather for its medicinal properties, of which there are many. The ancient Greeks used horseradish as an aphrodisiac, to ease back pain and to aid digestion after a rich meal – its pain-relieving and digestive uses are still commonplace (the use as an aphrodisiac rather forgotten). Allyl isothiocyanate, the oil that gives horseradish its punchy flavour, is also a powerful antibacterial compound which led to it being cooked with foul meat to make it safer to eat, and to mask the bad taste that no length of cooking could remove, leading to our tradition of eating roast meats with horseradish sauce.

Horseradish leaves are often mistaken for large dock leaves, but unlike dock they have serrated edges on their donkey-ear-like leaves, which again, unlike dock, grow straight out of the ground in large clusters. Gather young tender leaves for salads. Older leaves are best used in pureed sauces or fermented.

Push the leaves aside and you might see the stem attached to rhizome-like roots pushing above ground. The closer to the root, the more intense the levels of sinigrin.

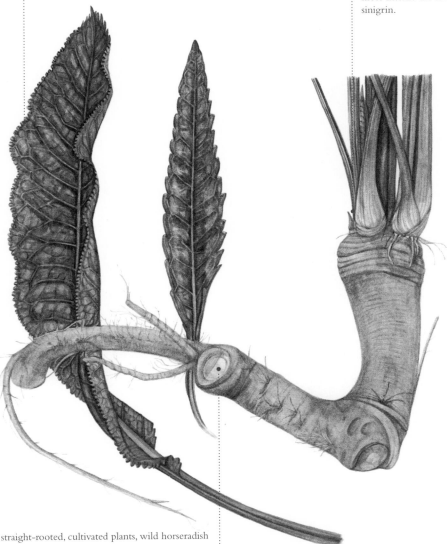

Unlike straight-rooted, cultivated plants, wild horseradish root is often gnarly and twisted, with a creamy ribbed skin that rubs away to expose the white flesh. Freshly dug whole roots smell mildly of the heat trapped within, which comes from sinigrin, a chemical in the plant that when exposed to the air turns into Allyl isothiocyanate, the flavour that we know gives heat to horseradish.

HORSERADISH

The mustard oil smell in horseradish is barely noticeable until the root is grated; when it is, the oils are released but swiftly lose pungency, turning bitter with time (vinegar halts the oil from losing flavour or turning bitter and is the ideal preservative to store horseradish in). Horseradish leaves and roots are best added at the end of cooking as heat reduces the pungency of the plant. Horseradish is used all around the world to add potent seasoning to dishes, from bread in Poland to pasta and *bollito misto* in Italy and is used as a bitter herb of Passover meals. The leaves of horseradish are bitter and peppery, like a hot rocket, when young. They are wrapped around breads in Poland and can be stuffed like dolma (see page 130).

HORSERADISH LEAF AND POTATO SALAD
Serves 4

- 100g tender horseradish leaves, pulled as close to the root as possible
- 20ml cider vinegar
- 1kg salad potatoes
- 2 garlic cloves, crushed
- 100ml olive oil, plus extra for drizzling
- 150ml Greek yoghurt
- 30g sorrel leaves (optional)
- Salt and freshly ground black pepper

Chopped young horseradish leaves create a sensational potato salad; an ideal recipe for those of us who don't have access to the roots but have found some leaves.

1. Grate the ends of the horseradish leaf stalks into the cider vinegar and leave to infuse while preparing the rest of the salad.

2. Scrub and steam the potatoes until tender and leave to cool. In another bowl, finely chop the horseradish leaf into grass-like strands, mix with the garlic, olive oil and yoghurt and add the stalk-infused vinegar. Season to taste and stir into the potatoes, then mix in the sorrel, if using.

3. Delicious served with eggs, mackerel or roasted beetroot.

HORSERADISH, BEETROOT AND CUMIN KHREN
Makes 600g

- 1 tsp white wine vinegar
- 1 tsp brown sugar
- 150g freshly grated horseradish
- ¼ tsp salt
- 450g roasted beetroot, grated
- 1 tsp cumin or dill seeds (optional)

Khren is a delicious condiment used in Jewish and Slavic food, either made in a white form, simply with horseradish and vinegar, or red with beetroot; they are traditionally dairy free. There are some variations: Central European horseradish sauces use sour cream whereas in Germany apples are added rather than beetroot.

1. Mix the vinegar, sugar, horseradish and salt in a bowl until well combined. Add the grated beetroot and cumin or dill, if using, and mix thoroughly. Pack into clean sterilized jars and store in the fridge for up to two weeks.

HORSERADISH AND TOMATO VODKA
Makes 750ml

- 50g horseradish root
- 750ml smooth vodka
- 100g dried tomatoes (not in oil)

Brought to America by German immigrants, horseradish was grown in the vegetable gardens of the influential, including George Washington and Thomas Jefferson, where it swiftly bolted the stable door and continued its gallop across its new home, growing wild and cultivated in farms. America is now the largest producer of horseradish in the world, with a fair amount of the roots ending up in fiery versions of Bloody Mary cocktails. This vodka infusion can be used in the iconic drink or stirred into tomato sauces to serve with pasta.

1. Finely slice the horseradish into matchstick-sized pieces and immediately cover with vodka in a wide-necked jar, then add the dried tomatoes and leave in a dark place for up to five days, strain and bottle. (The leftover tomato/horseradish mixture can be slowly heated with a tin of tomatoes to make a pasta sauce.)

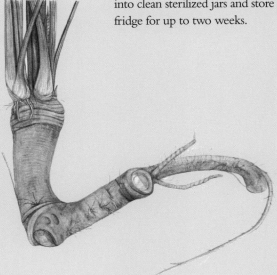

The flowers, opening from late spring until early autumn, are formed by numerous trumpet-shaped florets to create a round head that is usually 2–3cm wide, ranging in colour from pale mauve to reddish purple. Gather flowers on dry days when freshly opened and brightly coloured. Either use while fresh or thoroughly dry them immediately after harvesting, then store in an airtight container. Dried clover flowers can be used in herbal teas or ground into a powder to add to baking.

Lower growing clover leaves grow in a collection of three leaflets, forming a classic shamrock shape with a distinctive pale chevron marking each of the leaves. Older leaves are longer and more oval growing from the main flowering stem.

Caution: Clover should be avoided by people who are pregnant, nursing, or who have hormone-sensitive conditions or are on blood-thinning medication. When drying clover, ensure that it is done thoroughly, as soon as the plant is harvested, then store in a dry place in an airtight container. Avoid gathering from plants that have white powdery mildew on them.

Red clover plants have hairy stems and can grow up to 50cm tall, but when grown in mown areas are often shorter.

RED CLOVER

Trifolium pratense

⬢ DISTRIBUTION

Native to Europe, East Asia and Africa, introduced to most temperate regions of the world.

⬢ HABITAT

Hay meadows and grasslands, in garden lawns, on verges and waysides.

⬢ GATHERING SEASONS

Mid-spring–midsummer:
Leaves and tender stalks.

Late spring–early autumn:
Flowers.

Punctuating farmland, gardens and grassy verges with their ball-like flower heads, clover is a ubiquitous flower of summer, one of the plants responsible for the iconic smell of fresh hay meadows.

Clover was first cultivated over 1,000 years ago in Moorish Andalucía, where the wild plant was introduced into agriculture for its incredible 'nitrogen fixing' abilities – it absorbs nitrogen from the air and converts it into soil-enriching compounds, which grew healthier plants for food. Over the next 700 years its use spread across Europe, helping to enrich soils that had become depleted by increased demand on the land from growing populations. What appears to be an unassuming flower radically changed how we farmed; clover enabled Europe's population to grow nitrogen-hungry crops such as potatoes, it nourished cows to produce richer milk and attracted more bees, which in turn produced more honey, providing nutrition for a swiftly growing population. So important was clover that wherever people went, they took the seed along with them, and now all temperate areas of the world are covered with sweet clover.

Alongside its nitrogen-fixing properties, clover is rich in protein, calcium, vitamins A, C and the B-complex and also, importantly, contains isoflavones, plant-based oestrogen compounds which help regulate female hormones. Not only is clover important in supporting food production, it is a food in its own sweetly scented right.

RED CLOVER

Gather fresh clover on sunny days in early summer for its sweet and pea-like flavour. Fresh flowers add honeyed floral flavour to cakes, poached fruits, vinegars and drinks. The nutty, pea flavours of clover flowers are delicious used with savoury ingredients such as cucumber and radish, peanut satay sauces or scattered on honeydew melon salads with slices of Andalucían *jamon*, giving a nod to the plant's agricultural origins.

MIDSUMMER CLOVER CAKE
Makes 8 slices

- 10g dried clover flowers
- 200ml whipping cream, whisked to soft peaks
- 50g icing sugar
- 5 free-range organic eggs, separated
- 150g caster sugar
- 130g plain flour
- Pinch of salt
- Summer fruit jam, for spreading
- 200g cherries and/or strawberries, sliced
- Fresh clover flowers, to decorate

Midsummer in Scandinavia is celebrated with *jordgubbstårta* – a vanilla-infused cream and fruit layer cake. Replacing vanilla with dried red clover creates a sweet and wild dessert.

1. Grind a handful of dried clover flowers to a fine powder using a pestle and mortar and stir into the whisked cream in a bowl with 25g of the icing sugar, then chill until required.

2. Preheat the oven to 190°C, 375°F, gas mark 5. Grease and line two 20cm cake tins.

3. For the cake, whisk the egg whites until fluffy. In another bowl whisk the caster sugar with the yolks until doubled in volume. Sift the flour and salt into the sugar and yolk mix and carefully stir in, then gently fold in the egg whites. Divide the mix between the cake tins and bake for 12–15 minutes or until golden. Leave to cool before removing from the tins.

4. Thinly spread a summer fruit jam on one of the cooled cakes, then top with half of the cream and some sliced strawberries or cherries. Place the second cake on top, spread over the rest of the cream, then decorate with fresh clover flowers and dust with the remaining icing sugar.

RED CLOVER AND PEA POD DRESSING

Makes 500ml vinegar and 100ml pea pod oil

For the vinegar:
- Enough fresh clover flowers to fill a 500g jar
- 500ml apple cider vinegar
- 75g unrefined sugar or lightly flavoured honey

For the pea pod oil:
- 100ml light olive oil
- 100g peas in their pods (frozen peas are fine if you do not have fresh)
- Pinch of salt

Pairing the sweetened, floral vinegar with clover's legume relative, pea, makes a delightful dressing.

1. Place the clover flowers and vinegar in a food processor and blend to a purée and leave to infuse for 30 minutes before pouring the mixture through a sieve lined with a muslin cloth into a jar. Stir in the sugar or honey, tasting to make sure the vinegar is sweetened but sharp. Pour into a sterilized bottle and store until needed.

2. For the pea oil, place the olive oil, peas and salt in a food processor and blend to a purée. Leave the mixture to settle before passing through a fine sieve into a jar with a lid. Use a ratio of 1:3 vinegar to oil, before shaking the jar to mix the dressing, adding more vinegar and salt if required.

STIR-FRIED CLOVER LEAVES WITH TOFU – CAO TOU

Serves 4

- 200g extra firm tofu, cubed
- 4 tsp soy sauce for the tofu, plus 2 tsp for stir-frying
- 3 tbsp vegetable oil
- 400g clover leaves and tender stalks (pea shoots also work well alongside the clover)
- Pinch of salt
- 4 tsp rice wine or Baijiu spirit, to serve

Tender young clover leaves are wilted as a Shanghainese springtime speciality. They are highly nutritious but can cause bloating if eaten in excess, so use them as a side dish rather than as your main meal ingredients.

1. Preheat the oven to 190°C, 375°F, gas mark 5.

2. Toss the tofu in soy sauce. Heat 1 tbsp of oil and fry for 5 minutes, then transfer to the oven for 15 minutes until crisp. Meanwhile, wash and dry the clover leaves and stalks.

3. Heat the oil in a wok, add the leaves and stir-fry for 10 seconds, then add the salt and soy and cook for a further 20 seconds, until the clover has wilted.

4. Serve with the tofu and a dressing of rice wine or Chinese Baijiu spirit.

BIENNIALS

Biennials are plants which live for two years. During the first year, a seed germinates, growing a cluster of often low-lying leaves, and a root which acts as an energy store to produce vigorous growth, flowers and seeds in the following year. Many of these energy-filled first years' roots are rich in nutrients, and provide foragers with a winter source of carbohydrates.

EVENING PRIMROSE

Oenothera spp.

● **DISTRIBUTION**
Worldwide, native to
South and North America,
introduced to Europe
and Asia.

● **HABITAT**
Sunny, dry wastelands, coastal
areas, sand dunes, meadows
and gardens.

● **GATHERING
SEASONS**

Late winter–early spring:
Roots from first-year growth.

Spring:
Second-year shoots.

Summer:
Flower buds, flowers, fruiting
seed heads, leaves.

Late summer:
Ripe seeds.

Jars full of capsules of evening primrose seed oil fill pharmacy shelves, reached for by women across the world to help regulate female hormones. In its labelled bottles, evening primrose is one of the best-known and most widely used herbal remedies. However, in the neglected areas behind shops you will often find the plant itself; unidentified and unappreciated, yet offering the benefits of the capsules in deliciously perfumed food form.

The yellow-flowered, scented plant is native to North and South America where it has been used for thousands of years in a wide range of medicinal treatments, from wound healing to skincare. Early European settlers were enamoured by the plant and its powers. Just as they brought plants to the Americas, they also brought others back to Europe, introducing evening primrose into botanical gardens. The unassuming spire-like plant opens into bloom just after sunset, releasing a fragrance that lent it a name of 'wine scent', attracting moths and people to its sweet perfume. So enchanted were the romantically inclined European gentry that pre-theatre drinks parties were held to witness the spectacle. Of course, tastes trickle down and evening primrose self-seeded across Europe. Soon ordinary people saw the sweet yellow spires appear in their gardens, but rather than just gaze at the plant, they started eating it. A wise move, it turned out, as the plant is full of GLA (gamma-linolenic acid) fatty acids, responsible for healing and hormone balancing – and one of the reasons why you might well have a jar of seed oil in your bathroom cabinet today.

All evening primrose species have four petals; common evening primrose has heart-shaped, bright yellow petals surrounding a yellow pollen-covered stamen. The flower's perfume is released most powerfully at dusk. Flowering buds have a slight pepperiness.

Caution: Do not use if you are on blood-thinning medication or have low calcium or epilepsy.

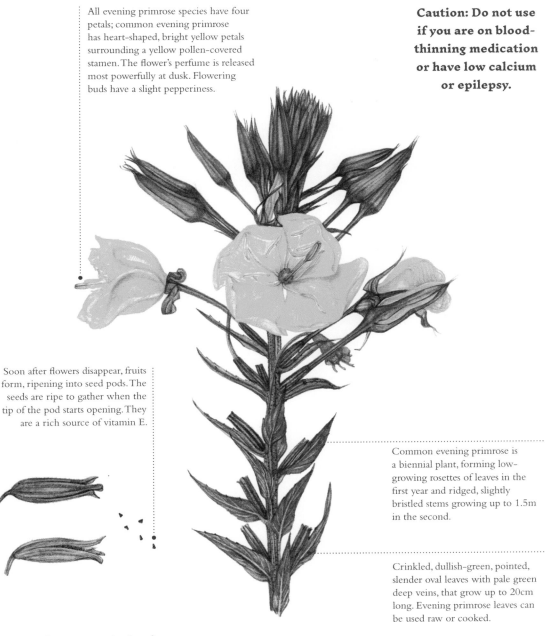

Soon after flowers disappear, fruits form, ripening into seed pods. The seeds are ripe to gather when the tip of the pod starts opening. They are a rich source of vitamin E.

Common evening primrose is a biennial plant, forming low-growing rosettes of leaves in the first year and ridged, slightly bristled stems growing up to 1.5m in the second.

Crinkled, dullish-green, pointed, slender oval leaves with pale green deep veins, that grow up to 20cm long. Evening primrose leaves can be used raw or cooked.

Large taproots the size of a parsnip can be gathered from late winter to early spring when tender and peppery; tasting like a cross between turnip and parsnip.

EVENING PRIMROSE

The mildly peppery, pink-tinged roots have a parsnip-like sweetness. They can be served boiled or fried, finely sliced and added to stir-fries. The leaves taste like mild turnip tops; quick wilting turns them into summer versions of spring greens. The petals and newly formed seeds have a beautiful perfumed taste, similar to jasmine; gather in the evening and infuse in syrups, liqueurs or cream-based puddings.

EVENING PRIMROSE SYLLABUB
Serves 4

- 100ml sweet white wine
- 30g caster sugar
- Zest and juice of 1 lemon
- 2 handfuls of freshly opened evening primrose flowers, gathered in the evening (about 30g)
- 300ml whipping cream

Legend attributes evening primrose's botanical name to Greek origins – *oinos* and *ther* meaning 'wine' and 'wild animal', from the fact that it would supposedly domesticate wild animals who ate the plant if it had been macerated in wine. You can macerate evening primrose flowers in sweet wine to make a syllabub; traditionally these were frothy drinks made with creamy milk and herb-infused sweetened wine. Delicious served with thin biscuits and fruit compotes.

1. In a pan, warm the wine and sugar and simmer, stirring occasionally, until the sugar has dissolved. Remove the pan from the heat and cool slightly, then add the lemon juice. Place the flowers in a jar with the sweetened wine, making sure the flowers are completely covered. Press a disc of greaseproof paper on top to prevent the flowers rising above the wine and oxidizing. Leave the flowers overnight, then strain them out through a fine-mesh sieve in the morning, reserving the infused wine.

2. Place the infused wine into a mixing bowl and slowly drizzle in the whipping cream, whipping vigorously with a balloon whisk until the mixture forms soft peaks. Do not over-whisk or the cream and wine will curdle.

3. Spoon into individual bowls, sprinkle with a fine grating of lemon zest and chill until ready to serve. Syllabub will keep, covered, for up to 2 days in the fridge.

EVENING PRIMROSE PASTE

Makes enough to fill a 120g jar

- 5 tbsp evening primrose seeds (add poppy seeds if you do not have enough evening primrose seeds)
- 2 tbsp honey or sugar
- 4 tbsp milk
- 2 tsp fresh lemon juice
- Pinch of salt
- ½ tsp vanilla extract (optional)

Evening primrose seeds can be swapped for any recipe calling for poppy seeds and, like evening primrose, poppy seeds are another delicious source of omega-rich oils and linoleic acids. This sweet paste is a twist on an Eastern European poppy seed delicacy, delicious simply spread on bread, and is also a versatile baking ingredient stirred into cake batters and biscuit doughs, or used in place of poppy seed paste in Eastern European breads and pastries.

1. Finely grind the seeds in a coffee or spice grinder. Add the powdered seeds to a saucepan with all the other ingredients. Heat, stirring continuously, and simmer for a few minutes until a thick paste has formed – it is ready when a trail forms as a spoon is dragged across the bottom of the pan.

2. Cool and keep, covered, in the fridge for up to 5 days or freeze in ice-cube trays until needed.

ROASTED EVENING PRIMROSE ROOT

Serves 4

- 8 large evening primrose roots, washed
- Juice of ½ lemon in 500ml water
- 3 tbsp olive oil
- 1 glass of white wine
- Salt and freshly ground black pepper
- 4 sprigs of thyme or parsley, chopped, to serve

Evening primrose root has a delicate pink hue to its flesh and can be cooked like parsnip, turnips or salsify – roasted, mashed or sweated. In France, the roots were served with ham, and the plant became known as *jambon de Saint Antoine* – after it was dedicated appropriately to the patron saint of pigs.

1. Preheat the oven to 180°C, 350°F, gas mark 4.

2. Peel and cut the roots lengthways, and place immediately into the lemon water. Once all the roots are prepared, drain and place them in a roasting tin, then toss in olive oil, season with salt and pepper and pour over the glass of wine.

3. Cover the tin with baking paper and a well-fitting lid and cook for 30 minutes. After 20 minutes, remove the lid to allow the roots to crisp on the edges.

4. Serve scattered with finely chopped thyme or parsley, and with a green salad and ham to make Saint Antoine proud.

GARLIC MUSTARD

Alliaria petiolata

❧ DISTRIBUTION

Native to Europe,
North Africa and Asia,
introduced to North
America and Australia.

❧ HABITAT

Garlic mustard thrives
in sheltered areas with
damp soil, by hedges,
woodland margins,
riverbanks and clearings.

**❧ GATHERING
SEASONS**

Late winter–early spring:
Young, tender leaves and roots.

Mid–late spring:
Tender stems, leaves, flowers
and newly forming seed heads.

Summer:
Mature, dark seeds.

Autumn:
First-year leaves.

Crushing the leaf of garlic mustard invites no mystery as to the flavour it holds; garlic, onion and mustard pulled together within one plant. If there was a flavour-pairing specialist of the plant world, garlic mustard is a contender for the title, cleverly featuring the tastes of some of the most commonly used flavours played with in modern-day kitchens.

Our recipes may be modern, but playing with flavours and adding spice to food is something far more ancient, as shown by the discovery of garlic mustard seeds pounded into the stone of a 6,000-year-old Danish cooking pot. Garlic mustard seeds are pungent and spicy and would only have been added for flavour; the stone pot contained within it the earliest recording of spicing for flavour – what were the 6,000-year-old chefs flavouring? Remains of fish bones next to the pot pointed to a feast of mustard and fish; a tradition that continues in Scandinavia today.

Neolithic Danish cooks used garlic mustard for its spice, and across Europe and Asia people treasured the vitamin A- and C-rich leaves for their medicinal properties and delicious flavours. The Europeans' penchant for garlic mustard led to it being taken by settlers to America, landing in Long Island in 1860. In its new home garlic mustard found a mixed welcome; arriving in a land where it had no predators, it spread unhindered throughout North America. Its rampant growth was helped by allelopathy – a clever ability that some plants have to produce a chemical that prevents others from germinating near it. Forests, clearings and pathways became dense with thickets of the white-flowered plant, which was regarded as so useful, delicious and treasured for so long in one continent, but became damagingly invasive in another. If you're looking to control its spread, take inspiration from the culinary artists of 4,000 BC, and eat it.

In the first year of growth, seedlings emerge in early spring, creating rosettes of heart-shaped leaves with scalloped edges. Young leaves are peppery and tender enough to eat raw; as they mature they develop more bitter flavours that are suitable for cooking or fermentation.

Long, thin seed pods turn papery when the seeds blacken and ripen. Tender pods can be pickled, the seeds used as a wild mustard spice.

In the second year of growth, flowering stems grow up to a metre in height. Clusters of four-petalled white flowers often appear alongside newly forming seed pods, which look like tender spikes around the flowers. The flowers are mild and peppery, delicious in salads.

Caution: If garlic mustard is invasive in your area, take care not to unwittingly spread the plant by carrying seeds on your shoes.

The first year's taproot has a pungent taste like a mild horseradish or wasabi; as it matures it becomes buttery and saltier in flavour.

GARLIC MUSTARD

Thick taproots can be puréed to make a horseradish-style sauce, or grated over food as a final pungent flavouring. Garlic mustard leaves are suited to many uses: they can be added to mint sauce recipes, crisped with oil, turned into pestos, fermented or blanched and frozen for winter use when they can be added to hummus, quiches, soups and omelettes. The leaves are equally tasty in Italian cabbage soups or Indian-influenced dishes. Large colonies of the plant will produce enough flowering stems to gather and eat like broccoli.

GARLIC MUSTARD GREENS WITH SPINACH
Serves 4

- 250g garlic mustard leaves and tender stems, washed and coarsely chopped
- 500g spinach, chard or fat hen leaves, washed and coarsely chopped
- 1 tsp turmeric
- 1 green chilli, finely chopped
- 1 tsp salt
- 1 tbsp finely grated fresh root ginger
- 6 tbsp ghee
- 170g cornmeal (maize flour)
- ½ tsp cumin seeds
- Pinch of asafoetida powder
- ¼ tsp red chilli flakes

Garlic mustard grows across northern India and is often used alongside other mustard greens in the region's food. The bitterness of garlic mustard is balanced with other greens such as spinach or fat hen.

1. Put all of the washed, chopped greens into a large saucepan with the turmeric, green chilli, salt and ginger, adding 250ml water, then cover and cook for 20 minutes, stirring regularly to make sure the leaves don't burn – add more water if it starts to dry out. After 20 minutes, add 4 tablespoons of the ghee. Mix the cornmeal with a cup of water to create a thin batter and add to the greens, stirring regularly for a further 20 minutes until creamy.

2. In a heavy-based pan, heat the remaining ghee and fry the cumin, asafoetida and chilli flakes for 30 seconds. Add the ghee and spices to the cooked greens, stir in, and serve with roti or flatbreads.

GRAPE AND GARLIC MUSTARD MUSTARD

Makes enough to fill a 350g jar

- 25g garlic mustard seeds
- 25g brown mustard seeds
- 25g yellow mustard seeds
- 100ml red wine
- 200ml red wine vinegar
- 50ml red grape juice (or grape must, if you have some available)
- 1 tsp salt

The ancient Danish mustard-loving cooks used the seeds they collected as a spice, but it took the Romans to turn the mustard family seeds into a sauce; they blended grape must (the skins of pressed grapes) with ground seeds to create *mustum ardens*, or 'burning must', which led to the name 'mustard' and the sauce we all know today. This recipe is a nod to the original mustard sauce, using red wine vinegar, wine and red grape juice to make a punchy, violet-hued condiment to slather on sandwiches and serve with roasts.

1. In a lidded container, combine the seeds, salt, wine and vinegar so that the seeds are totally saturated by the liquid. (Add more vinegar or wine if required) Cover the mixture with baking paper to ensure all the seeds are under the liquid, replace the lid and leave at room temperature for two days.

2. Place the seeds, red wine and vinegar liquid into a food processor with the grape juice and purée until creamy. Taste and add more grape juice if the sauce is not sweet enough. Transfer to a sterilized jar with a tightly fitting lid and leave to mellow for a week before using.

GARLIC MUSTARD REMOULADE

Serves 4

- 2 tbsp mayonnaise
- 2 tbsp crème fraîche or natural yoghurt
- 2 garlic mustard roots, grated into 100ml apple cider vinegar and infused overnight
- 100g young garlic mustard leaves and tender flowering stems, finely chopped
- 400g peeled celeriac or turnips and radishes
- Juice of ½ lemon
- Pinch of sugar (optional)
- Salt and freshly ground black pepper

Remoulade originated in France, traditionally made with garlic mustard's relative, horseradish. Soaking young roots of garlic mustard in apple cider vinegar highlights their similarity in flavours.

1. Mix together the mayonnaise, crème fraîche or yoghurt and 2 tablespoons of the garlic mustard root-infused vinegar. Stir in the finely chopped leaves. Using a mandolin, shred the celeriac into matchstick-thin pieces and toss into the dressing. Leave for 30 minutes for the flavours to develop, then taste and season with salt, pepper, lemon juice or a pinch of sugar if required.

2. Serve piled onto bread, or with ham or fish.

BURDOCK

Arctium spp.

❧ DISTRIBUTION

Across all temperate regions of the world.

❧ HABITAT

Most soils, woodland edges, meadows, gardens, flower beds, wasteland.

❧ GATHERING SEASONS

Autumn–spring:
Roots of first-year growth.

Spring–early summer:
Stems and leaves.

Summer–autumn:
Seeds.

Wherever people are, burdock usually isn't far away; the astute plant evolved seed pods covered with little bent hooks that cling. There's a reason burdock might remind you of a certain ubiquitous hoops and loops fastener – the inventor of Velcro, George de Mestral, was inspired by the cleverly sticky seeds as they clung to his dog's coat following a woodland walk. When burdock seeds are ripe, you will also find them sticking to shoes and clothes; unlike Velcro, the burrs are so adept at sticking to anything that you could also find them clinging to bare skin. This is the reason why wherever people or animals live or roam, you will find burdock growing. As we travelled, they came with us across continents, and even on long journeys across oceans, hiding in the wool of livestock being moved to new lands.

Burdock may be a hitchhiker, but it gives us plenty in return for its lift. A member of the sunflower family, burdock is an excellent immune regulator, renowned for blood cleansing and supporting the liver and feeding our gut flora, as well as being rich in dietary fibre, calcium, potassium and amino acids. After we carried it to its new home, burdock would set seed and provide us with a valuable carbohydrate-rich harvest. The roots and stems have been used in food and medicine for thousands of years, and until recently they were gathered and eaten all across Europe and Asia. But the plant has fallen out of favour and is now mainly the preserve of Asian nations, where it is cultivated and treated as the incredibly useful vegetable it really is – almost as useful, in fact, as Velcro.

In the second year of its life, burdock sends up tall stems and from these grow smaller flower stems. The stems are covered in an incredibly bitter substance, which needs to be peeled away to reveal the more palatable flesh of the inner stem. The leaves can be used to make bitters for cocktails.

Burdock roots are best harvested at the end of their first year of growth, before the second year's main stem starts forming. Dig a wide margin around the plant and carefully dig down into the ground exposing the thick taproots. Burdock roots snap easily, so take care when digging them out of the ground.

Burdock flowers grow like globe artichokes on prickly balls, pale purple in colour, and provide an important food source to pollinating insects in late summer. The fruits (or seeds) that form once the flower goes over are used in herbal skincare preparations.

Caution: Burdock can be confused with butterbur, which has much rounder leaves and distinctive reddish-violet flowers growing like cones from the base of the plant. Burdock can occasionally cause dermatitis in people with sensitive skin.

Burdock's thick leaves grow up to 50cm long. In the first year of growth, the downy, wavy-edged leaves form a low-growing rosette, coming from a long carbohydrate- and inulin-rich taproot.

BURDOCK

Burdock is best known in culinary usage for its roots, which are widely eaten in Asian countries, but its above-ground parts are equally as nutritious and delicious. Dug up at the end of the first year's growth, the large roots should be peeled and scrubbed to remove bitterness, leaving a mild, crisp and slightly sweet root that can be eaten raw, cooked or dried for later use. Japanese recipes are extensive, including braising in soy, or pickling.

BURDOCK FRITTERS
Serves 4

- 250g young burdock main stem, and young flowering stems
- 2 tsp salt, plus extra to season
- 50g plain flour
- Pinch of freshly ground black pepper
- 1 egg, lightly beaten
- 1 tbsp water
- 25g Parmesan, grated
- Light olive oil, for frying

Cardoon- and artichoke-loving southern Italians migrated to the United States in the early 1900s, only to discover that these bitter plants did not grow in America. However, burdock did, having set up home there a few hundred years earlier. Soon burdock stems were used in place of cardoon in Italian-American food, and it became known as *carduni*, or wild cardoon.

1. Discard any discoloured outer stalks and small leaves from the burdock. Peel and trim the stems, removing strings from stalks with a vegetable peeler and completely peeling away the thick outer layer of the main stem. If the stems taste bitter, soak them in a bowl of water with the salt for a couple of hours.

2. Place in a pan, cover with water and simmer until the stems are tender (usually 20–25 minutes). Drain and allow to cool. Mix the flour and pepper together in a shallow bowl and in another bowl, whisk the egg, water and cheese. Toss a quarter of the burdock stems with the flour, then dip them into the egg mixture, making sure the stems are fully coated, but letting any excess drip away. Carefully place the stems in a shallow frying pan of hot olive oil, turning them as they cook, until golden on all sides. Drain the cooked stems on kitchen roll, season with salt and serve immediately.

DANDELION AND BURDOCK CORDIAL

Makes 500ml

- 10g dried burdock root or 50g fresh root
- 10g dried dandelion root or 50g fresh root
- 5cm piece of fresh root ginger
- 1 star anise, crushed
- Peel of 1 organic orange
- 250g sugar
- 100ml black treacle

Originally created in medieval Britain, tales tell of heavenly inspiration leading to St Thomas Aquinas making the first dandelion and burdock drink in 1265. Whether it came about due to divine inspiration or not, the British people took to it religiously, and hundreds of years later the liquorice-flavoured drink can still be bought in the least wild of supermarkets.

1. Place the roots, star anise and orange peel in a pan and cover with 500ml water. Keep on a gentle heat, barely simmering, for about 30 minutes. Strain through a muslin cloth and return to the pan, then mix in the sugar and treacle and heat, stirring, until dissolved. Once cool, pour into sterilized bottles and refrigerate until needed.

2. The cordial is best diluted 1:5 with soda water, or can be used to flavour ice cream, cakes and biscuits.

CARROT AND BURDOCK KIMPIRA

Serves 4

- 250g burdock root
- 250g carrots
- 2 tbsp sesame oil, plus extra to serve
- 1 tbsp brown sugar
- 175ml dashi (or water if you are vegetarian)
- 3–4 tbsp light soy sauce
- 3 tbsp mirin (rice wine)
- ½ tsp black sesame seeds

Kimpira is a widely cooked Japanese vegetable dish that can be eaten warm or kept in the fridge and served chilled. You can buy burdock roots in most specialist Japanese shops, where the root is often labelled as *gobo*.

1. Peel and wash the burdock and carrots, cutting them into thin strips, or juliennes. Heat the sesame oil in a frying pan, then add the burdock and carrots and sauté for a few minutes. Add the brown sugar and dashi (or water) and soy sauce and cook for about 10 minutes. Add the mirin and continue cooking until the liquid has nearly all evaporated.

2. Transfer to a serving bowl and sprinkle with more sesame oil and the sesame seeds. Serve with rice or greens.

Caution: As it is a member of the carrot family great care must be taken when identifying hogweed. Fresh hogweed contains a sap that can cause blistering to the skin before it is cooked, gather hogweed using gloves.

The flowering buds of hogweed are aromatic and delicious, tasting similar to purple sprouting broccoli. However, the buds open to form large flat clusters of white flowers growing in umbels, up to the size of an opened hand. They have a distinctly unpleasant 'public toilet' smell, and are best left to the insects that pollinate them.

Large hairy leaves growing from the ground and up from the main stems are divided into between three and five sections; the shape of the leaves can be irregular, and you will need to use other features to ensure correct identification. Giant hogweed leaves have a pointier, more ragged-looking appearance than common hogweed's rounded leaves.

Hogweed grows up to around 2 metres high, and sometimes taller. Its slender grooved, hollow stems are covered with coarse bristles. The stems vary in colour from purple to dull green but never blotchy.

Each pollinated flower forms oval, flattened fruit, up to 1cm in length, growing upwards from the stem with two fine fibres growing at the tip, like antlers. The green fruit soon ripens into papery seeds. The fruits have a citrus, cardamom flavour and can be pickled or infused in liqueurs; dried seeds develop hints of mace, coriander seed and orange and are used as a spice in sweet and savoury dishes.

COMMON HOGWEED

Heracleum sphondylium

◗ **DISTRIBUTION**

Native to Europe, North Africa, East Asia and North America.

◗ **HABITAT**

Moist, nitrogen-rich soils – verges, hedgerows, waste ground, woodland.

◗ **GATHERING SEASONS**

Early–late spring:
Emerging shoots, roots.

Mid-spring–midsummer:
Flower buds.

Midsummer–mid-autumn:
Seeds.

Imagine a plant that provides spring food so delicious that not only its new shoots have chefs falling over themselves with excitement, but also its perfumed flowering buds and, fruits and finally, seeds whose flavour rivals the most expensive of exotic spices you can buy. A plant that was this adaptable and delicious surely must be one of the most sought-out, prized ingredients? Not quite. Hogweed might be one of the best wild foods there is, yet it has a reputation that is far less appealing: as a misunderstood member of the carrot family.

Each summer, cases of hogweed 'poisoning' are slathered over newspapers, with images of nasty blisters on arms, legs and faces after people have encountered it and its big brother, giant hogweed. The sap within hogweed (and in far greater quantities in giant hogweed) contains furocoumarin, a chemical that causes phytophotodermatitis, making skin very sensitive to light, resulting in blisters on exposed skin. But it isn't only hogweed which causes this – garden-grown parsnips can cause the same condition, but we don't demonize parsnip and we eat the roots with abandon.

Because of the sap, hogweed does require careful harvesting, but judicious gathering with gloves and washing your hands afterwards will prevent burns. Heating kills the active part of the sap that causes burns; just like dried beans and potatoes, hogweed needs cooking to make it edible, but that shouldn't scare you off gathering it, as it is one of the most incredible flavours of any food, wild or cultivated. Once you try hogweed, you will in all likelihood understand why chefs all around the world go weak at the knees when trays of hogweed arrive in their kitchens; only you'll have the added benefit of fine dining for free.

COMMON HOGWEED

Young hogweed shoots are beautiful wilted in oil then finished with butter, salt and a squeeze of lemon juice. The young buds and unopened florets have a flavour reminiscent of purple sprouting broccoli and kale and can be interchanged for these in recipes. Hogweed shoots, leaves and stems are fermented as vegetables and drinks and the perfumed roots can be eaten as a vegetable similar to parsnip or infused into gin.

HOGWEED BORSCHT
Serves 4

- 2 litres beef or vegetable stock
- 2 bay leaves
- 1 garlic clove
- 1 tsp black peppercorns
- 3 beetroots
- 1 large onion
- 4 medium tomatoes, cut in half
- 3 large carrots
- Olive oil, for cooking
- 12 hogweed shoots
- 100g sauerkraut, rinsed of its juices, or fermented hogweed
- 50g sorrel or rhubarb in ribbons
- 100ml sour cream
- A handful of dill, chopped
- Boiled eggs or shredded beef, to serve

The famous, deep-red beetroot soup was originally green – made with fermented hogweed stems. This version pairs the now familiar purple beetroots with the original green leaves.

1. In a saucepan, heat the stock with the bay leaves, garlic, peppercorns, one of the beetroots, the whole onion, tomatoes and one carrot. Cover and gently simmer for 30 minutes. Remove any scum from the top of the stock as it cooks, then, when cooked, strain through a fine sieve and return to a clean pan and keep warm.

2. Meanwhile, using a vegetable peeler, slice the remaining beetroots and carrots into ribbons, then toss in olive oil with the hogweed shoots, add to a pan and sweat, with the lid on, until soft. Add the sauerkraut or fermented hogweed and sorrel or rhubarb at the end of cooking to heat through.

3. Pile the vegetables into a soup bowl, pour over the hot stock, add a spoonful of sour cream and scatter with chopped dill. Serve with boiled eggs or shredded beef.

ADVIEH HOGWEED SEED PERSIAN SPICE MIX

Makes 60g

- 20g dried hogweed seeds
- 5g black peppercorns
- 5g cardamom seeds
- 5g mace
- 5g coriander seeds
- 5g cumin seeds
- 10 cloves
- 5g ground cinnamon
- 5g ground ginger

Like many plants, different species grow in different climates and soils across the world. The form of hogweed that grows around the Caspian Sea is known as Persian hogweed, or golpar. Golpar seeds are frequently used as a spice in Persian food, sprinkled into tagines, over pomegranates, broad beans and rice and in chutneys. They are often ground with salt to make a popular seasoning known as *namak*. Advieh is a Persian spice mixture which often contains hogweed. This blend is delicious in both sweet and savoury dishes.

1. Place all of the whole spices in a spice grinder and grind until powdered, then stir in the cinnamon and ginger. Store in airtight glass jars until needed.

HOGWEED PARKIN

Serves 8–10

- 110g butter
- 75g black treacle
- 170g dark brown soft sugar
- 150g fine oatmeal (or ground porridge oats)
- 75ml milk
- 200g self-raising flour
- Pinch of salt
- ½ tsp ground ginger
- 3 tsp coarsely ground hogweed seeds
- 1 large egg, beaten

Parkin is a traditional spiced cake made in northeast England, often served in November at Guy Fawkes Night. Hogweed's earthy aromatic flavour is delicious in parkin, capturing a sweet essence of autumnal days, and the last of hogweed seed harvesting.

1. Preheat the oven to 160°C, 325°F, gas mark 3. Melt the butter over a low heat in a heavy-based pan. Add the treacle and sugar and stir occasionally until dissolved. Remove from the heat and stir in the oatmeal and milk, then gradually add the flour, salt, ginger and 2 teaspoons of the hogweed seeds. Finally, fold in the egg.

2. If the mix is too thick, add a little more milk until you have a thick but pourable mix. Pour into a greased and floured 20cm cake tin and cook for 1 hour or until a fork comes away clean after being pushed into the centre of the cake.

3. After baking, cool and sprinkle with the remaining ground hogweed seeds.

THISTLE

Cirsium spp.

❧ DISTRIBUTION

Native to Europe, West Asia and northeast Africa, thistles have naturalized across the world.

❧ HABITAT

Cultivated fields and meadows, verges, garden borders and longer lawns.

❧ GATHERING SEASONS

Winter–spring:
First-year plant roots.

Late spring:
Young stalks, first year basal leaves.

Summer:
Tender central stems, flowers.

Late summer–early autumn:
Dried flowers, seeds.

In the story of the expulsion from the fertile Garden of Eden, God cursed the land that Adam and Eve were sent to with 'thorns and thistles'; from then on, thistles are peppered through the Bible as symbols of desolate, infertile ground. You will indeed find thistles growing in the poorest soil, but the curse wasn't as bad as it seemed, because where thistles really thrive is in deep, rich soil – under the field of prickles you're more likely to find fertile lands than biblical bleakness.

The spines of thistles hide other incredibly alluring traits and benefits to ecology and people. Plants with armouries of prickles or stings are often defending themselves from being over-grazed, and once you discover the delicious, mild, celery flavour of the stems and leaf mid ribs – high in fibre, protein, phosphorous, magnesium, calcium, copper and zinc – you'll see why defence is needed.

Thistles are biennials, growing large, deep roots in the first year. After its first season of growth the roots can be gathered and eaten as a vegetable; they are rich in inulin, a carbohydrate that nourishes healthy gut bacteria and is thought to lower cholesterol levels. Thistle flowers are one of the most nectar-rich plants in existence, providing a late summer buffet for vital pollinators, followed by essential energy-rich seeds for migrating birds, including finches and linnets. The seeds are rich in omega oils and silymarin, a flavonoid that helps support and protect liver cells from damage – the very reason why people reach for milk thistle after particularly unpuritanical nights on the town.

A plague on the Earth? A curse? Adam and Eve had less to worry about than they might have thought.

All thistles have spiny bracts at the base of their flowers. The flowers are usually purple, occasionally white or yellow; they are delicious in syrups, baking or liqueurs. Thistle flowers are also used as a rennet, which splits milk to make cheeses and yoghurt. All thistles produce hairs attached to omega-rich seeds.

Before flowering, the inner flesh of a thistle stem is like mild celery. Using gardening gloves, peel back the top layer of thistle to reveal vibrant green beneath; it becomes too tough to eat raw as it ages, but it can still be cooked into soups and sauces.

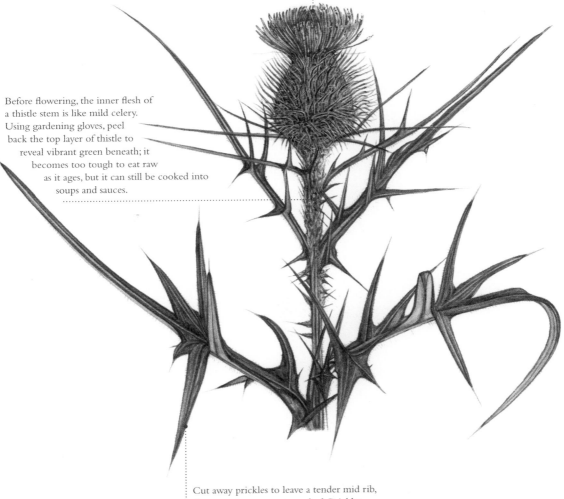

Cut away prickles to leave a tender mid rib, that you can eat raw or cooked. Prickles on thistles will not soften even with long cooking, but they can be used in teas.

Cirsium vulgare

THISTLE

Thistle stems are eaten in North Africa and the Mediterranean region; bundles of young plants with their prickles cut away are a seasonal delicacy at markets from Portugal to Morocco. The stems are delicious sweated in oil and dressed with lemon, served as an antipasto like thistle's relative, the artichoke. The flowers of thistles vary in scent and flavour, some tasting like honey, others floral. Stronger-flavoured flowers can be infused into honey and jellies and used as edible flowers on sweet and savoury dishes; snip the flowers off the plant and use immediately or dry for later use.

THISTLE APERITIF
Makes 750ml

- A cup of perfumed thistle flowers
- 1 tsp honey
- 650ml Moscato or other sweet wine
- 10cm piece of artichoke, cardoon or burdock leaf
- 100ml brandy

Cardamaro is a flavoured wine traditionally made with bitter cardoon leaves, thistle and a range of botanicals, then aged for at least six months in oak barrels to produce a sweetly bitter liqueur. To make a quicker, more floral drink, the sweetness of thistle flowers works beautifully in a dessert wine like Moscato; and the bitterness from the burdock or artichoke leaf makes this honeyed drink a perfect pre-meal sip.

1. Place the flower petals and honey in a 1-litre jar, pour over the wine, then stir and seal.

2. Place the artichoke, cardoon or burdock leaf in another jar with the brandy, seal and leave both jars in a dark place for 24 hours.

3. Strain the liquids through a sieve into a jug, discarding the leaves and petals, and blend the wine and brandy together. This drink is best used fresh but can be stored in the fridge for a couple of weeks. Serve as an aperitif, with a mixer such as apple juice, or in cocktails with whiskey or apple brandy.

BRAISED THISTLES WITH ALMONDS

Serves 4 as a starter

- 20 tender thistle stems, peeled
- 150ml olive oil
- 2 garlic cloves, finely grated
- 100g ground almonds
- ½ tsp salt
- 200ml water
- 30g parsley, chopped
- 1 tbsp capers

Thistles are served in Spain with nuts, fish and pork. The mild flavour of thistle goes incredibly well with almond and garlic sauce. To prepare the thistle stems, peel back the young tips of thistle to reveal the tender inner stem, cut into 10cm batons, and toss in olive oil with a squeeze of lemon juice as soon as the outer layer has been removed, to prevent the thistle turning brown.

1. Add the thistles to a heavy-based pan and slowly braise in the olive oil until soft.

2. Remove the soft stems from the oil and place in a serving dish. Add the garlic, ground almonds and salt to the pan, adding enough of the water to create a sloppy sauce, then stir over the heat until thickened. Pour the liquid over the thistle stems and scatter with chopped parsley.

3. Scatter with capers and serve with bread as a starter.

THISTLE AND TOMATO SAUCE

Makes a 400g jar

- 100g sliced good-quality stale bread
- 100g tender, peeled thistle stems (see Thistle and Almond Sauce recipe for directions)
- 300g ripe tomatoes, roughly chopped
- 1 garlic clove, peeled
- 2 tbsp wine vinegar
- 50ml extra virgin olive oil
- A pinch of each of salt, ground coriander, cumin seed, black pepper, chilli flakes and paprika

Thistle stems are frequently made into pâtés and sauces in the Mediterranean region. In Sardinia they are blended with bread and oil in a tapenade-style sauce, and in Cadiz thistles (also known as *tagarninas*) are turned into a pâté-style sauce known as Picarnina, which can be stirred through stews, or served on bread or with grilled meats, fish and vegetables.

1. Lightly griddle or toast the bread. Once cool, chop it into 1cm cubes. Place the bread cubes and all of the other ingredients into a food processor and blend to a coarse purée.

2. Transfer to a clean jar, seal, and store in the fridge for up to 1 week.

ANNUALS

Annuals grow from seed to mature plant within one season, sometimes producing more than one generation of plant in a year. Reliant on ensuring the next generation of plants is successful, many annuals have unique seed dispersal strategies – from the clockwork mechanism of Himalayan balsam to the sticky seeds of cleavers. Annuals often grow in large clusters, producing vigorous growth suitable for the wildest of salad bowls.

CHICKWEED

Stellaria media

Chickweed is one of the most common plants growing across the
world. Its stems trail across the ground, forming mats of lush green
foliage under the dappled shade of trees and in garden beds. If you
have a garden, you are most likely to have chickweed growing in it.

Chickweed's name comes from its use as a nutritious food for
chickens and other farmed birds, but it's not just domesticated
birds that feed on this plant; wild species across the world rely on
chickweed seeds as an important food to support them on long
journeys. Chickweed can set seed all year, but it prefers the cooler
months to flower and produce seeds, keeping birds nourished during
the winter.

Chickweed has not only sustained winged travellers, but also those
who travelled by boat. Chickweed was one of the armoury of plants
used to prevent scurvy caused by lack of fresh food on long ocean
voyages; it was infused into vinegars to provide a mineral-rich
tonic for sailors and migrants heading for America. Packed full of
nutritional virtues – rich in iron, vitamins C, B-complex, A and a
wide range of minerals and trace elements – chickweed has been used
for centuries as a nutritionally dense food, often turned into tonic
drinks for people who are rundown and ill.

Chickweed leaves have a mild nutty flavour with hints of sweetcorn, suitable for eating raw or lightly cooked.

Fine line of hairs along one side of the stalks. The tips of stems are often tender enough to eat raw in salads; when older they become stringy, developing a fibrous 'inner tube' that pulls out of the stem when broken. Older leaves and stems are best puréed into pestos and soups.

Small leaves that grow in pairs opposite each other. The leaves fold up around young flowering buds at night, to protect the tender buds.

Small white flowers, 1cm across, with notched petals and yellow/green stamens, which grow at the top of leaf axils. Seeds and flowers can be eaten raw or cooked.

Caution: Chickweed can be confused with the toxic scarlet pimpernel, which has small orange-red flowers and square stems. To prevent confusion, gather chickweed when it is displaying its white flowers.

CHICKWEED

Chickweed grows across the world, and has been used by many cultures as part of their folk medicine and food for thousands of years. Dense in nutrients, yet with a mild flavour, it is an easy plant to add to everything from salads to pestos.

CHICKWEED SAUERKRAUT
Makes 1kg

- 800g white cabbage
- 200g chickweed (a colander bowl full)
- 1 tsp cumin, caraway or dill seeds, or dried chilli flakes
- 1½ tbsp pure sea salt (without caking agents or other preservatives)

Sauerkraut is fermented using naturally occurring lactic acid, which gives it and pickles and kimchi their distinctive tang.

1. Thoroughly wash the cabbage and chickweed, then coarsely chop the chickweed and finely slice the cabbage. Place both ingredients and any flavourings into a large, clean bowl. Sprinkle with the salt and, with clean hands, massage the salt into the chickweed and cabbage for 5 minutes. Rest for a few minutes before massaging again, then squeeze out the liquid from the vegetables. This liquid is your brine, so do not throw it away.

2. Pack the vegetables into a sterilized jar or fermenting crock, squeezing them down. Cover with the brine, pressing the vegetables down again to make sure that any air bubbles are expelled and that the vegetables are completely submerged under the liquid. (Add a cabbage leaf or a bag filled with water to the top to help keep the vegetables from being exposed to air.)

3. Seal the jar and put in a dark place at room temperature. Loosen and retighten the lid each day to relieve the pressure build-up created by carbon dioxide – a by-product of fermentation. The sauerkraut will be ready to eat after 4–5 days but its flavours will intensify if it is allowed to ferment fully – this can take anywhere from 2 to 6 weeks. Full fermentation is indicated when the brine stops producing bubbles.

4. Taste the sauerkraut every few days after this point, and once the flavour is to your liking, place the jar in the fridge to slow down fermentation.

CHICKWEED, BLACKBERRY AND LENTIL SALAD
Serves 4

- 50g blackberries
- 1 tsp honey
- 1 tsp French mustard
- 1 garlic clove, minced
- 1 tbsp apple cider vinegar
- 3 tbsp extra virgin olive oil
- 50g tender chickweed tips
- 2 shallots or 1 red onion, finely diced and soaked in water for 10 minutes
- 1 uncooked beetroot, finely shredded
- 25g fresh green hazelnuts or toasted hazelnuts
- 250g cooked and chilled Puy lentils
- Selection of herbs – fennel, dill, oregano, marigold and basil work well in this salad
- 100g feta cheese, crumbled
- Salt and freshly ground black pepper

The earthy flavour of Puy lentils is a perfect ingredient in autumnal food, alongside the deeply flavoured blackberry juices. This salad is delicious served with sour cheeses such as feta, or seared seasonal wood pigeon or venison (or an equally delicious last barbecued sausage of the year).

1. Make the dressing by crushing half the blackberries with the honey, mustard, garlic, cider vinegar and olive oil. Season with a pinch of salt and black pepper. Toss the chickweed tips, soaked shallots or onion, beetroot, nuts and lentils in the dressing. Pile into bowls and scatter with the herbs and remaining berries and feta.

2. Serve with warm breads and a glass of something as red as the dressing.

SEVEN-HERB RICE PORRIDGE – NANAKUSA
Serves 4

- 200g Japanese short grain rice
- 1 litre water
- 50g freshly gathered chickweed, finely chopped
- Nanakusa herb mix (available dried from a Japanese supermarket, alternatively you can use a fresh blend of herbs of your choice, finely chopped)
- Salt

In Japan, 7 January is celebrated as the Festival of Seven Herbs, when people eat rice porridge accompanied by seven kinds of the first wild greens of the year, which includes chickweed.

1. Place the rice in a sieve and rinse under running water until the water runs clear. Soak the rice in a bowl of water for 30 minutes, then drain and rinse for a second time in a sieve until the water runs clear.

2. Place the rice and the water in a pan, cover with a lid and bring to a boil over medium-high heat. When it is boiling, stir the rice, cover, lower the heat and simmer for 25–30 minutes (don't lift the lid or stir the rice). After 25 minutes, remove from the heat and let steam for 10 minutes. Add the herbs, season with salt to taste and serve.

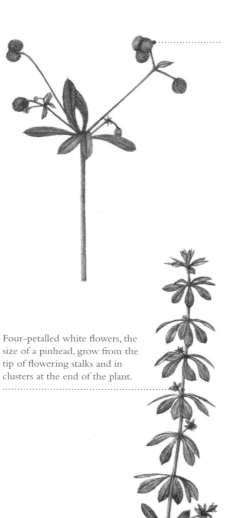

Pairs of small round fruits covered in hooks, soft and green when young, ripening to dark, hard seed pods. Related to the coffee plant, cleaver seeds can be roasted and used as a mildly caffeinated drink.

Groups of 6–10 narrow leaves grow around the main stems, spaced up to 5cm from the next set of leaves. Short flowering stems grow between the leaves, with sets of smaller leaves at the ends.

Tiny bristles along square stems.

Four-petalled white flowers, the size of a pinhead, grow from the tip of flowering stalks and in clusters at the end of the plant.

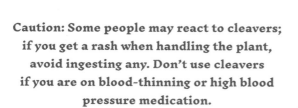

Caution: Some people may react to cleavers; if you get a rash when handling the plant, avoid ingesting any. Don't use cleavers if you are on blood-thinning or high blood pressure medication.

CLEAVERS

Galium aparine

If you spent any time outside as a child you probably stuck a stem of cleavers on someone's back – if you didn't do it, you possibly weren't outside enough. Cleavers are one of the most recognized of weeds because wherever people live, so do they – like burdock, their cunning ability to stick or cling to anything that passes by is an ingenious way of spreading seed, especially when the seed in question needs to grow in nitrogen-rich soils such as those that surround human habitation.

Tasting grassy, herby and fresh, cleavers start growing just as most other foliage dies back in the winter, sending up thin little shoots that provide nutritious food during the coldest months. Cleavers are rich in vitamin C, calcium, sodium and silica, and have a long history of being used in herbal medicine both for their diuretic and anti-inflammatory properties. Another benefit of the cleaver is its ability to improve the function of our lymphatic system (a network of nodes, ducts and glands that help eliminate waste and toxins from cells, and send bacteria-fighting immune cells around our bodies). A food that supports our lymphatic system in the winter is one to be cherished. Whether or not you spent enough time outside as a child, cleavers are well worth heading outside for.

CLEAVERS

Fresh cleavers are delicious in both hot and cold drinks; to make a cold cleaver tonic, add stems to a jug of water and refrigerate overnight to allow the benefits of the plant to infuse into the water, and pour into your water bottle to drink the next day. Warming cleaver tea is best made with water that has cooled slightly after boiling – pour it over the cleavers and allow to steep for 10 minutes.

CLEAVER COFFEE MOUSSE
Serves 4

- 50g unrefined sugar
- 10g cleaver coffee powder
- 4 gelatine leaves, soaked in water (or a vegetarian alternative)
- 4 large free-range eggs, separated
- 220ml whipping cream, whisked until stiff
- 25g dark chocolate, to decorate

Cleavers and coffee are both members of the Rubiaceae family of plants, and the seeds of cleavers contain a small amount of caffeine and taste mildly like coffee. Ground, roasted cleaver seeds are often drunk as the closest replacement to coffee you will find. Pick the burrs (seeds) when they are ripe or turning brown, dry them out by placing them on a clean cloth on a radiator and then roast at 120°C, 250°F, gas mark ½ until the seeds darken. Grind the seeds to a powder to make coffee or add to this mousse.

1. Heat the sugar in a pan with 110ml water and the cleaver coffee powder over a medium heat, stirring occasionally, until boiling and the sugar has dissolved, then take off the heat and leave to infuse overnight.

2. The next day, strain the cleaver coffee syrup through a fine cloth into a pan, then reheat until the syrup is hot. Squeeze any excess liquid from the gelatine leaves and add to the pan, stirring well until the gelatine has dissolved completely. Beat the egg yolks in a heatproof bowl until light and creamy. Whisk the egg whites until stiff in another bowl. Pour the cleaver mixture over the egg yolks and, using a large metal spoon, gently fold in the egg whites, alternating with spoonfuls of the whipped cream. Spoon into individual bowls and place in the fridge for at least an hour or until set. Using a vegetable peeler, peel flakes of dark chocolate over the pudding.

RHUBARB AND CLEAVER SPRING REVIVER

Makes 750ml

- 1kg rhubarb, washed and chopped into 5cm chunks
- 300g sugar
- 10 juniper berries
- 100g cleavers, washed
- Thumb-sized piece of fresh root ginger, finely sliced

Bright pink stems of indoor grown (or 'forced') rhubarb come into season just as cleavers are full of vitality in the later winter months. Both rhubarb and cleavers are renowned for their blood-purifying tonic properties, and together with the warming spices of ginger and juniper they make a sensational reviving drink that's perfect for late-winter sipping.

1. Place the rhubarb in a wide pan, cover with 750ml water and set over a medium heat. Simmer until it is pulpy and has given its colour up to the water.

2. Strain the rhubarb (all is not lost for the fruit – you can add the pulp to apples to make a crumble), and pour the liquid through a muslin cloth into a measuring jug, topping up the liquid with water until it measures 500ml. Pour into the pan, add the sugar, and heat until the sugar has dissolved. Once the juice and sugar has turned into a clear syrup, turn off the heat and allow the liquid to cool before pouring into a jug with the juniper berries, cleavers and ginger. Infuse overnight, then strain out the cleavers, ginger and juniper and heat the liquid to boiling point before pouring into a sterilized bottle. The mixture can be kept in the fridge for up to 2 weeks.

3. Serve diluted with sparkling water or tonic and a splash of restorative gin.

WILTED CARROT AND CLEAVER WINTER SALAD

Serves 4

- Light olive oil or hazelnut oil
- 2 large handfuls of young cleaver shoots, washed and dried
- 4 large carrots, peeled and grated
- 1 tsp ras el hanout or ground cumin
- Squeeze of lemon juice or a drizzle of good apple cider vinegar
- Salt

Carrots and cleavers share earthy flavours and are great bedfellows in a wilted salad; wilting removes any of the rough texture from the plant without cooking out the goodness.

1. On a low heat, add a glug of oil to a wide pan, add the cleavers and carrots with a splash of water and the ras el hanout or cumin, cover and cook for 5 minutes, until the cleavers start to wilt.

2. Taste and add a squeeze of lemon juice or a splash of cider vinegar to give a subtle zing, season with a sprinkle of salt and leave to cool to room temperature.

3. Serve with flatbreads and curd cheese, or chicken thighs with apricots and almonds.

HAIRY BITTERCRESS

Cardamine hirsuta

● **DISTRIBUTION**

Native to Europe and Asia, introduced almost globally except in Antarctica.

● **HABITAT**

Damp, disturbed soil, flower beds and often in potted plants.

● **GATHERING SEASONS**

Late summer–late spring: The whole plant is available throughout the year (until hard frost) but it is least flavoursome in the heat of summer.

Across temperate regions of the world, many countries have a period in early spring known as the Hungry Gap, when locally grown fresh greens and fruit are hard to find. With our supermarket shelves full of food from thousands of miles away, many people will be unaware of the lack of local produce in their diet at this time of year, but try to harvest your own food from a vegetable patch in early spring and the lack of edible ingredients is all too clear to see.

Yet what you will find in place of leafy cultivated crops at this time of year will often be rosettes of wavy-leaved, white-flowered bittercress – sometimes this will be growing compact as a micro herb, other times expanding to the size of a lettuce – thriving through autumn until late spring. Most gardeners wish to see the back of bittercress, diligently removing the shallow-rooted weeds from their otherwise empty beds, whilst sighing and wondering when fresh salads and delicious mineral-laden greens will be growing again, unaware that this is exactly what they are pulling up. One nibble on a bittercress leaf has most horticulturalists converted, regretting the years of backache they have endured pulling up the delicious, versatile vegetable they have been accidentally cultivating. Crammed full of high quantities of vitamin C, calcium, magnesium, beta carotene and antioxidants, bittercress is the harvest we crave during the lean months. The weed that thrives in the winter, it turns out, contains the goodness we need. Early spring is hungry no more.

The little seed pods are tender
enough to eat for a few days, turning
woody quicker than most plants.
When ripe, the slightest touch
triggers the long, thin seed pods to
explode, sending seeds flying feet
away from the original plant.

Four-petalled, tiny white
flowers growing at the top
of flowering stems.

Hairy bittercress leaves grow
on short stems from a basal
rosette. The plant can remain
small, with only a few
leaf stems, or grow up to
30cm wide, similar to frisée
lettuces. Each leaf stem has
numerous pairs of roughly
heart-shaped leaflets that
grow opposite each other
along the stem. The tiny
flowers make delicious mild
garnishes.

HAIRY BITTERCRESS

Bittercress's mildly peppery and broccoli flavour makes it a versatile ingredient – add tender young leaves and flowers to salads; coarser older leaves can be finely chopped into frittatas, puréed into pestos and added to chimichurri sauces and salsas. If large enough, the roots can be finely chopped or puréed with a mild oil.

GRIDDLED PEAR AND BITTERCRESS SALAD
Serves 4

- 2 firm pears
- Juice of 1 lemon
- 100g stale white bread, torn into bite-sized pieces
- 30g shelled walnuts
- 2 tbsp light olive oil
- 100g tender bittercress
- 100g rocket
- 50g chicory or young dandelion leaves

For the dressing:
- 3 tbsp olive oil
- 1 tbsp fruit vinegar (damson or blackberry are ideal)
- 1 tsp French mustard
- Salt and pepper to season

To serve (optional):
- 50g Manchego cheese
- 25g quince membrillo, cut into cubes

Bittercress produces vibrant new growth in the autumn. Given that you'll often find it thriving in orchards, you can gather salad and fruit at the same time.

1. Cut the pears into quarters, remove the cores, put the flesh into a bowl and squeeze over the lemon juice. Heat a frying pan over a high heat, then add the pears and cook for 2–3 minutes. Turn over the pieces and cook the other side. When the pear is charred but still firm, remove from the pan and set aside.

2. Toss the bread and walnuts in the oil, season with salt and toast in the pan until crisp and golden.

3. Mix the dressing ingredients together in a bowl and season to taste. Add the salad leaves and toss to coat in the dressing.

4. Serve the leaves with the warm pear quarters, croutons and nuts. If using, shave over the Manchego cheese and scatter with the cubes of quince membrillo.

BITTERCRESS MASHED POTATO

Serves 4

....

- 1kg potatoes, peeled and chopped into bite-sized chunks
- 250ml single cream
- 3 tbsp butter
- 1 tsp salt
- Finely chopped garlic
- 1 tsp thyme
- 100g bittercress, very finely chopped
- 1 tsp horseradish sauce (optional)

....

There is little that is more comforting on a bleak winter's day than mashed potato. With the addition of vitamin C-laden bittercress, indulgent mash becomes more virtuous and quite delicious when served alongside a gravy-rich beef or mushroom casserole.

1. Add the potatoes and a good pinch of salt to a pan and just cover with water. Cook until tender, then drain until dry.

2. In another pan, warm the cream with the butter, salt, garlic and thyme and leave to infuse for 10 minutes before straining out the garlic.

3. Mash the potatoes in the warmed cream mixture. Once smooth, stir in the bittercress and leave for a couple of minutes. Add a dollop of horseradish sauce if you would like a more peppery bite.

CHILLI AND BITTERCRESS SALSA

Makes 200g

....

- 75g bittercress leaves and tender stems
- 3 tbsp red wine vinegar
- 1 shallot
- 2 garlic cloves, minced
- 2 tbsp oregano leaves
- 1 medium-heat red chilli, finely chopped
- 135ml olive oil
- Salt and freshly ground black pepper

....

The vibrant peppery flavour of bittercress works well with the heat of chilli, and older, less tender leaves and stems can be used in sauces like chimichurri if they are puréed to a fine consistency.

1. Add the bittercress, vinegar, shallot garlic, oregano and chilli to a food processor or mini blender and process until finely chopped. Season with salt and pepper.

2. Transfer to a bowl and stir in the olive oil. Leave to infuse for at least 30 minutes before using. Delicious on grilled meats and vegetables.

Leafless flowering stems grow like spikes from the basal leaves. Round and slender, they are covered with many tiny greenish flowers growing around the top half of the stem. Once ripe, the egg-shaped seeds can be easily stripped away from the stem. Often the husk will also come away and can be eaten along with the seed.

Thick stems join at the base of the plant, with veined leaves growing in rosettes close to the ground; often growing up to 20cm in height. The fleshy leaves have a mushroomy, mildly nutty flavour and can be eaten raw when young, or cooked as they get older.

Caution: Avoid eating large amounts of plantain if you have a blood-clotting disorder or are on blood thinners.

Plantago major

PLANTAIN

Plantago spp.

DISTRIBUTION

Originally from Europe
and Asia, now global. There
are around 200 species of
Plantago, many of which
are edible.

HABITAT

Paths, cultivated land,
gardens, parks.

**GATHERING
SEASONS**

Late spring–mid-autumn:
Leaves.

Midsummer–late autumn:
Seeds.

When European settlers travelled to the Americas and Australia they
took with them broadleaf plantain seeds. Many of the seeds were
unknown cargo, within the earth-laden ballast of the ships, stuck to
livestock, boots and the edges of clothes, but some of the seeds would
have been taken on board intentionally as important parts of the
medicinal toolkits of migrating families. As Europeans landed in both
continents and established settlements, so plantain put down its roots
and started to march across the land. So vigorous was the advance and
impact of these European people and their plant across America and
Australia that First Nations' people in both continents named plantain
'White Man's Footprints'.

This, however, was not the first time that plantain followed people's
footsteps. Ever since people began to live in settlements, synanthropic
plants like plantain moved from the forests to live alongside us. A
synanthrope, from the Greek words meaning 'together with man', is
an animal or plant that thrives where people live; plants benefit from
nitrogen-laden cleared and disturbed ground that is enriched with our
waste, which creates an irresistible environment for nitrogen-loving
plants to establish and thrive. Synanthropic plants often grow with
vigour, so much so that they become viewed as invasive, unwanted
weeds. Yet the weeds that grow near people are often edible, and the
nitrogen-rich soil enables them to absorb vast amounts of nutrients,
becoming valuable food within arm's reach. Plantain is amongst the
best of them: rich in fibre, vitamins C, A and K, along with minerals
including calcium, copper, potassium, magnesium and zinc, and a
range of beneficial antioxidants. Its medicinal value is of equal worth:
from soothing burnt, stung or irritated skin to supporting digestive,
respiratory, bone, eye and immune health. The weed that wanted to
set up home wherever we went perhaps should be treated less as an
uninvited guest and more as a welcome neighbour.

PLANTAIN

The distinctive mushroom and nutty flavour of plantain places this plant as a definite savoury ingredient; young leaves can be used in salads raw, or wilted as vegetables – no more than 5 minutes' cooking softens the leaves to become an ideal green vegetable. Crumbled leaves and seedheads can be added to creamy carbonara and stroganoff sauces to add flavour and nutrients.

PLANTAIN SEED AND NUT CRACKERS
Makes 25 crackers

- 3 tbsp pumpkin seeds
- 3 tbsp sunflower seeds
- 2 tbsp toasted hazelnuts
- 3 tbsp ripe plantain seeds and husks
- 3 tbsp sesame seeds
- 3 tbsp linseed
- ¼ tsp salt (or 1 tsp dried plantain stock mix)
- ½ tsp dried herb of your choice
- 250ml water
- 2 tbsp olive or hazelnut oil

Plantago species include the widely used psyllium, whose husks and seeds are sold in health food shops across the world. All plantains have seeds with the same mucilaginous, dietary-fibre-rich properties and are brilliant as nutritious binding agents. Gather seeds by stripping the ripe seed pods from the plant and separating seeds and pods through a fine-mesh sieve.

1. Place half of the pumpkin seeds and sunflower seeds, and all of the hazelnuts in a food processor and blend to a fine crumb.

2. Place all of the ingredients in a bowl and leave to stand for 10 minutes so that the plantain seeds can release their mucilaginous gel into the water. Vigorously stir the mixture, pressing into it to start bonding the mixture together.

3. Preheat the oven to 150°C, 300°F, gas mark 2. Line a large baking tray with baking paper and spread the mixture with a spatula evenly across the paper, so that it forms a layer 3–5mm thick. Place in the oven for 30 minutes, then remove and cut into individual squares. Return the tray to the oven for another 30 minutes, by which time the crackers should be crisp and lightly toasted. Leave until completely cold, then store in an airtight container.

PLANTAIN STOCK MIX
Makes 100g

- 150g fresh plantain leaves
- 100g leeks
- 100g fennel bulb
- 100g carrot
- 50g celery
- 100g onions
- 2 garlic cloves
- 3 tsp fine sea salt

Young plantain leaves are tender enough to add to salads, but as they get older they need to be cooked or dried. Their deeply savoury flavour and highly nutritious nature make them ideal to use in place of shop-bought stock cubes to season soups and sauces and flavour roasted vegetables.

1. Wash the vegetables and plantain and very finely slice the vegetables, then place the leaves and vegetables in a dehydrator or in an oven on its lowest setting until all the leaves and vegetables are fully dried.

2. Place the vegetables in a food processor and blend until they turn into a coarse powder. Crumble in the plantain leaves, add the salt and blend again. If the mixture starts to look damp this will be due to the salt drawing out any remaining moisture. (If this happens, spread the mix on a baking sheet and place in the oven, on its lowest setting, to dry out for 20 minutes). Store in an airtight glass jar in a cupboard for up to 6 months.

PLANTAIN AND MARIGOLD-INFUSED OIL
Makes 750ml

- 50g fresh plantain leaves
- 30g fresh marigold flowers (10g dried)
- 750ml olive oil

Whoever said 'Whatever you put on your body, you should be able to put in your body' was right. The peppery, earthy flavour of marigold flowers pairs incredibly well with plantain in food, as a dressing or cooking oil and as an herbal ally. Both plants are healing and soothing internally as well as externally and make a nourishing oil to moisturize dry, irritated skin.

1. Wash, dry and dehydrate the plantain leaves, along with the marigold flowers until the leaves and flowers are crumbly – which shows that no liquid is left in the plant. Put the dried leaves and dried marigold flowers into a jar, cover with olive oil and secure the lid tightly. Shake to coat the leaves and flowers in the oil and place the jar in a yoghurt maker, or in a slow cooker on its lowest setting, and cook for 8 hours. The herbs will become crisp, and the oil will absorb the flavour and soothing properties of the plants. Strain and store in a dark jar away from light for up to 6 months.

Flower spirals of white/green spikes that open to produce edible black seeds.

Caution: Fat hen contains oxalates, and is best consumed in moderation by anyone with kidney issues. Do not confuse edible fat hen with toxic nightshade plants, which often grow in the same conditions. Fat hen flowers are tiny and pale green, growing in clusters on spikes, nightshade flowers have five petals, and are white, yellow or purple.

Fat hen stems are hairless with darker green grooves that split off at leaf axils. Young tender stems can be used as a vegetable.

Fat hen belongs to a group of plants known as goosefoots – members of the amaranth family, their lower leaves often resemble goose footprints. When young, the triangular leaves grow opposite each other, their toothed edges and a dusting of wax crystals giving a powdery appearance. The leaves grow in small clusters up the main stem, which become slimmer higher up the flowering stem. Fat hen leaves can be eaten raw in salads, or wilted as a green vegetable.

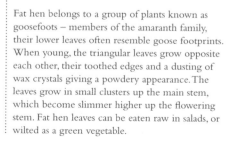

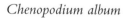

Chenopodium album

FAT HEN

Chenopodium spp.

Common as the muck heaps on which it grows, fat hen (often also known as lamb's quarters) is often found in farmyards and enriched fields, thriving on nitrate-rich soils and manure heaps. In some countries the fast-growing annual is met with open gathering arms, in others it is regarded as an invasive weed, contaminating crops such as spinach, quinoa and chard – its less easy to grow, less nutritious relatives.

Fat hen is one of the most nutritious plants in the world; rich in vitamins A and C, calcium, phosphorous and potassium. Its love of the nitrogen-rich soils that surround homes mean it is frequently just a few steps away from most people on the planet, providing sustenance in diets across Asia, South America and Africa. It is prized for its leaves, which wilt into the most delicious of greens, and protein-packed seeds: it is a super-abundant superfood.

Fat hen has only recently lost its edible reputation in Europe and America; before its tender cousin spinach was introduced from West Asia in the 1600s, fat hen was a valued vegetable in Britain and northern Europe – a position it had held for thousands of years. Eaten by Romans, Vikings and Saxons alike, fat hen was rebranded as a weed, resulting in the loss of a versatile and delicious vegetable. Now its reputation as a food has been forgotten in the West, but it keeps trying to creep back into our diets, pushing into cultivated crops, trying to regain a place at the table.

FAT HEN

Fat hen's nutritional prowess is matched by its fertility – each plant can contain tens of thousands of seeds, which can be eaten or left to grow and form mounds of wild tender greens the following spring. The tender new growth is the most delicious part of the plant, so if you treat it like a cut-and-come-again crop you will have a continual supply of leafy greens even when your spinach and chard have long bolted. The tiny black seeds may be microscopic compared to quinoa, but they pack an equally protein-laden punch, and are eaten roasted and coarsely ground, added to pancakes, muffins and breads.

FAT HEN FLATBREADS
Makes 6

- 200g fat hen leaves, washed and finely chopped
- 160g wholewheat flour
- 1 tsp minced garlic
- 1 tsp grated fresh root ginger
- 2 green chillies, finely chopped
- ½ tsp red chilli powder
- ½ tsp cumin seeds, toasted
- 1 tsp salt
- ½ tsp ground coriander seeds
- ½ tsp garam masala
- Vegetable oil

In India, fat hen (*bathua*) is grown as a food crop, and *bathua paratha* is a moreish herb bread that is made in the Punjab region. This delicious bread has equivalents in other areas of the fat hen growing world, too.

1. In a large bowl, mix together the fat hen, flour and flavourings. Slowly add enough water to form a soft dough. Knead for a minute, cover and let it rest for 10 minutes.

2. Divide the dough into six portions, then roll each into 10cm circles and heat a heavy-based frying pan. When the pan is hot, place a flatbread on it for 30 seconds, then turn it over and cook on the other side for 1 minute. Spread a small amount of oil on the flatbread before flipping it over again. Keep flipping until the flatbread is roasted on both sides, with brown char marks. Transfer to a warm plate and cook the remaining flatbreads. Serve with raita and pickles.

FAT HEN AND PINTO BEANS

Serves 3 as a main, 6 as a side

- 450g fat hen leaves and tender stems, rinsed
- 1 tbsp olive oil
- 2 tsp minced garlic
- 1 red chilli, finely sliced
- 3 medium leeks, finely chopped
- 400g tin of pinto beans, drained and rinsed
- Salt and freshly ground black pepper

In Mexico, wild green vegetables are known commonly as *quelites* – fat hen is known as *quelites cenizo* which means 'ash quelite', since the white coating makes it look like it has been dipped in ash. Fat hen is frequently eaten in South America and is often stewed with onion and garlic and served with beans or tortillas. Nutritious, fast and simple to make, this dish is perfect served as a side or a filling main.

1. Blanch the fat hen for 1 minute in a pan of boiling water, then transfer immediately to a bowl of ice-cold water. Drain, squeeze out the water and finely chop.

2. Heat the olive oil in a large pan and sweat the garlic, chilli and leeks until translucent and soft. Stir in the fat hen and beans; cover and cook for 5 minutes, then season with salt and pepper and serve.

FAT HEN AND FISH STEW

Serves 6

- 500g fat hen leaves, washed and finely sliced (you can bulk this out with spinach or chard)
- 1 medium onion, finely chopped
- 1 garlic clove
- 2 tomatoes, peeled and chopped
- 200g salted fish, soaked and flaked from the bones (traditionally this recipe used catfish but salt cod or haddock works well)
- 150g peanut butter
- 3 tbsp sustainable red palm oil or hazelnut oil

Fat hen grows abundantly across Africa, where it is known as wild spinach, and it is often used in stewed dishes, where the greens are added at the start of cooking rather than the end, creating a texture and taste that is unique to African cooking. This dish is based on *fumbwa*, a Congolese recipe, a dish traditionally flavoured with nutty red palm oil, a native plant to central and west Africa. You can replace the red palm oil with hazelnut oil, but if you choose to use red palm oil, be sure to use sustainably produced oil.

1. Place the fat hen, onion and garlic in a pan with 100ml of water, then cover and simmer until they have softened completely. Add the tomatoes and continue to simmer for 5 minutes. Add the fish and cook for a further 10 minutes. Finally, add the peanut butter and oil, stir into the dish and simmer for a further 10 minutes until ready to serve.

Orchid-shaped, sweetly scented flowers
vary from pale pink to bright cerise.
Providing pollen all summer, the flowers
are attractive to bees and edible for
humans – use in salads and infusions.

Teardrop-shaped fruit droop from
the ends of thin stems, containing
hundreds of seeds per plant, and coils
that project seeds metres from the
plant. The fruit and ripe seeds are
edible and nutty.

Pinky-red square
stems. Himalayan
balsam can grow
up to 3 metres
in a year.

Lance-shaped, toothed, shiny green
leaves with red ribs grow up to 25cm
long, sometimes in clusters of five
leaves, forming dense foliage that
shades out other plants.

HIMALAYAN BALSAM

Impatiens glandulifera

Balsam grows high in the Himalayas in little colonies scattered amongst other native plants; a beautiful punctuation of pink orchid-like flowers on slender stems. The elegant plant must have been alluring to the plant hunters who first plucked it from its homeland, proudly cultivating seeds in London's famous glasshouses at Kew. Little did the plant hunters know what a controversial and adaptable plant they were bringing home, as unlike other tender flowers, balsam needed no cosseting in heated glass buildings to thrive. The hardy flowering stems were incredibly adept at spreading away from gardens and across continents, aided both by gardeners and the plant's own clever seed dispersal mechanism. Growing coiled springs inside seed pods which ping ripe seeds up to 5 metres from the original plant, meant that within fifteen years of its arrival in Europe, Himalayan balsam had sprung out of manmade confines and back into the wild. Thriving on a lack of competitors or pests, Himalayan balsam produced thickets of plants, crowding out native species. Setting up home on riverbanks, the plants catapult seeds into waterways, where they float to their new homes, forming new colonies of pink in summer, growing such large clusters they can impede water flow. Then, as they die back in the winter, they leave swathes of riverbanks bare, vulnerable to erosion.

Himalayan balsam, like many beautiful plants from other climates, has become categorized as such an invasive species that planting it could land you with a hefty fine. However, you can play your own role in curbing its onward march by stopping the plant from spreading. As an annual, the plant is spread purely by seed dispersal. Gathering the flowers before they turn to seed prevents the formation of seeds and also provides an edible, drinkable ingredient. And should you discover that the flowers have already turned into tear-drop earring-like seed pods, place a jar over the pods and trap the catapulting seeds. Carefully lid your jar, check your clothes and shoes for any stowaway seeds and head home to enjoy your role in reining back the delicious invasive.

HIMALAYAN BALSAM

Before Himalayan balsam seeds, gather the flowers and use them in jams, jellies, syrups, or vinegars or infuse them into drinks such as gin.

The fruit pods containing forming tender seeds can be added to stir-fries or steamed as a vegetable. When the seeds reach maturity, they develop a nutty, slightly meaty taste. Grind raw seeds with oil and herbs to make pestos, add toasted seeds to spice blends and dukkahs, or scatter in salads, soups, curries, crackers, breads and cakes.

FIG AND HIMALAYAN BALSAM SEED JAM
Makes a 400g jar

- 250g sticky dried figs
- 125g sugar
- 250ml water
- Juice of ½ lemon
- Zest of ½ organic orange
- 25g Himalayan balsam seeds, toasted
- Pinch of ground cinnamon

Sweet, sticky figs grow wild in the Himalayas and combine with balsam seeds to make a beautiful jam full of crunch from the seeds of both plants. Eat the jam as a sweet conserve or with cheeses.

1. Roughly chop the figs (removing the stalks) and place in a pan with the sugar, water, lemon juice and orange zest. Heat to a simmer, stirring frequently for 20 minutes or until the figs become soft. Once the mixture has reduced and become thick and sticky, stir in the Himalayan balsam seeds and cinnamon. Spoon into sterilized jars, seal and store for up to 6 months.

HIMALAYAN BALSAM SALT AND PEPPER SEASONING

Makes enough to fill a 100g jar

- 2 tbsp Himalayan balsam seeds
- 1 tsp Sichuan peppercorns
- 1 tbsp finely ground pink Himalayan salt

Celebrating the immense Himalayan mountain range, this aromatic seasoning blend combines salt, pepper and seeds from the mountains that straddle Asia, and can be used as a rub or a seasoning for soups and sauces.

1. Preheat the oven to 120°C, 250°F, gas mark ½. Place the Himalayan balsam seeds on a baking sheet and roast in the oven until starting to become crunchy.

2. Meanwhile heat a heavy-based pan and dry roast the peppercorns and salt for a minute or so, until the peppercorns become aromatic. Take off the heat, and add the balsam seeds.

3. Once cool, grind to a rough powder using a pestle and mortar and store in an airtight container for up to 6 months.

HIMALAYAN BALSAM AND SUNFLOWER SEED BUTTER

Makes enough to fill a 120g jar

- 100g sunflower seeds
- ½ cup Himalayan balsam seeds
- Pinch of salt
- 1 tsp sugar

The nutty flavour of Himalayan balsam seeds complements sunflower seeds. This recipe can be used as a spread or as a tahini replacement in salad dressings.

1. Preheat the oven to 160°C, 325°F, gas mark 3. Line a large baking sheet with baking paper and pour on both sunflower and Himalayan balsam seeds. Roast in the oven for 10–20 minutes, until some of the seeds are lightly golden.

2. Cool, then place in a blender and process until smooth (this can take anywhere from 5–10 minutes). Add salt to taste, and a teaspoon of sugar if the butter has a slight bitter taste.

3. Transfer to an airtight container and keep in the fridge for up to a month.

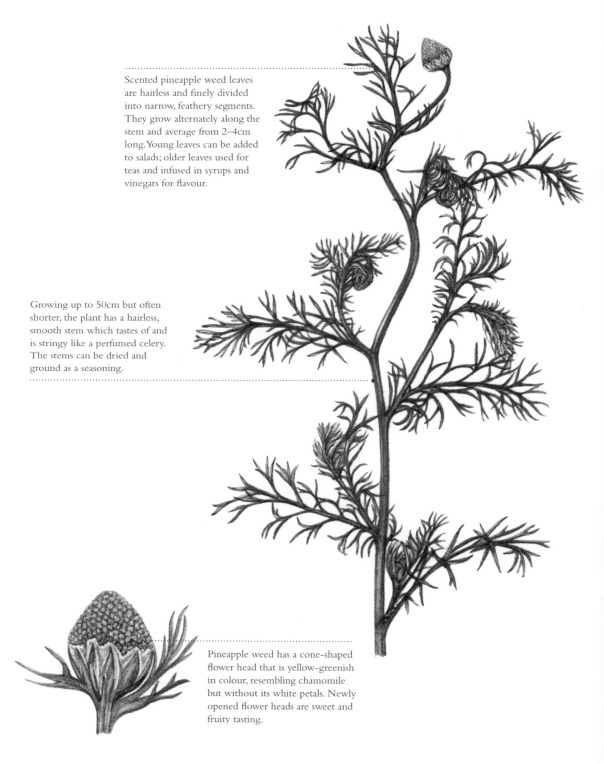

Scented pineapple weed leaves
are hairless and finely divided
into narrow, feathery segments.
They grow alternately along the
stem and average from 2–4cm
long. Young leaves can be added
to salads; older leaves used for
teas and infused in syrups and
vinegars for flavour.

Growing up to 50cm but often
shorter, the plant has a hairless,
smooth stem which tastes of and
is stringy like a perfumed celery.
The stems can be dried and
ground as a seasoning.

Pineapple weed has a cone-shaped
flower head that is yellow-greenish
in colour, resembling chamomile
but without its white petals. Newly
opened flower heads are sweet and
fruity tasting.

PINEAPPLE WEED

Matricaria discoidea

❧ **DISTRIBUTION**

Native to northeast Asia, now
in most parts of the world.

❧ **HABITAT**

Poor, compacted soil, often
on roadways, lanes and drives.

❧ **GATHERING
SEASONS**

Late spring:
Tender leaves and tips of stems.

Early–late summer:
Flower heads and tips of leaves.

Rough-trodden path gateways and compacted land turn in
midsummer from stony ground into scented green carpets of low-
growing, stunted-looking chamomile flowers with a delightful,
familiar scent – ripe apple maybe? Chamomile tea, perhaps? Sweet
pineapple? Definitely.

Pineapple weed originally grew in northeast Asia and as people
travelled, so did the plant. Its thousands of almost microscopic seeds
become sticky when wet and inconspicuously stowed away on the
soles of livestock, people and on wheels as they trundled past.

This astute means of hitching a ride, coupled with its quick life cycle,
ability to grow in poor compacted soil and tough stems helping
withstand the roughest of treatment meant that it found a home for
itself by roadways, the perfect location to hitchhike around continents.
One pineapple weed plant was introduced to Britain as a specimen to
London's Botanical Gardens in Kew in 1879, and within 25 years it
had travelled the roads, lanes and driveways across the country, to be
widely dispersed by the start of the twentieth century.

Pineapple weed's liking for growing and spreading via roadways has
unexpected benefits for people. It is closely related to chamomile,
and a quick infusion of pineapple weed tea is used to settle upset
stomachs, ease headaches and calm anxiety. Its calming properties are
thought to help with gentle release of energy – just the ticket on long
journeys by foot or in a car.

COOK & EAT
PINEAPPLE WEED

A sublimely flavoured herb, the young leaves and flowers combine a mixture of fruity apple and herbal chamomile flavours. Dried flower heads of pineapple weed can be used in similar ways to chamomile, in soothing, anti-anxiety teas, especially to aid rest at night-time, and to provide a calm boost in the morning. The exotic fruity taste of the fresh leaves and flower heads taste beautiful in savoury and sweet dishes alike. They can be used fresh, infused in salads, sodas, jellies, liqueurs, granitas and panna cottas.

PINEAPPLE WEED POACHED APRICOTS
Serves 4

- 30g dried pineapple weed
- 200g sugar
- 500ml sweet dessert wine
- 20 fresh apricots, cut in half and stone removed
- 200ml double cream, whipped
- Finely chopped fresh flower heads and tender leaves, to garnish

The beautiful summer fruit is sensational when flavoured with pineapple weed. Roasting intensifies the taste of the fruit and creates a deeply flavoured syrup that can be drizzled into sparkling wine, to make a clear, wild Bellini.

1. Pour 500ml of water into a large, heavy-based ovenproof pan, and bring to the boil. Add the pineapple weed and sugar, remove from the heat and leave to infuse for 30 minutes.

2. Preheat the oven to 140°C, 275°F, gas mark 1.

3. Strain the syrup, return it to the pan with the wine and bring back to a simmer. Add the apricot halves, cover with baking paper and a lid and place in the oven for 20 minutes or until the apricots are tender. Remove from the oven and leave to cool.

4. Slip off the skins from the apricots and leave to steep in the syrup for 4 hours. Stir a couple of teaspoons of the cooking syrup through whipped cream, and serve with the apricots, scattering over finely chopped fresh flower heads and tender leaves.

PINEAPPLE WEED
HERB BLEND

Fills a 250g jar

- 30g dried pineapple weed flowers
- 15g dried thyme
- 15g dried oregano
- 5g ground fennel seeds

Pineapple weed occupies the edges of agricultural land, and its scent is equally close to that of dried hay; hay-flavoured herb blends are the natural seasoning for pasture-fed meats and are also delicious used to flavour tomato and cream sauces, focaccia breads and hay-scented syrups.

1. Rub together all of the herbs and use to season food as you would herbes de Provence, just with a more meadow flavour.

PINEAPPLE WEED AND
CUCUMBER LIQUEUR

Makes 200ml

- 4 tbsp pineapple weed flowers
- 175ml good-quality vodka
- 100g cucumber, grated (skin on)
- 100g sugar

Pineapple weed appears as quickly as burning summer heat replaces the lushness of spring. Cucumber and pineapple weed make for an incredibly cooling pair to soothe the most wilted of travellers.

1. Place the pineapple weed flower heads in a wide-necked jar with the vodka, then let it infuse for 2 hours. As soon as the vodka has taken on the flavour of the flowers, strain through a fine sieve or muslin cloth. After straining the flowers, add the cucumber to the vodka, and leave to steep overnight.

2. The next day, strain the cucumber, and make a simple syrup: put the sugar and 100ml of water in a pan and bring to a boil, then cook over a medium heat, stirring, until the sugar has dissolved. Cool, then add 50ml of the syrup to the infused vodka, stir and taste, adding more syrup if required.

3. Pineapple weed liqueur is beautiful served with iced soda water or in summer punches such as Pimm's.

RED DEAD NETTLE

Lamium purpureum

❧ DISTRIBUTION

North and South America,
Europe, Asia, Australia, Japan.

❧ HABITAT

Disturbed land, roadsides,
gardens, meadows and fields.

**❧ GATHERING
SEASONS**

Late winter–late spring:
Young shoots and flowers.

Early autumn–late winter:
Second growth of shoots
and flowers.

The mint family includes over 3,500 plants – from garden mints to other widely used but less obviously minty herbs, such as basil, sage, rosemary and lavender. Edible mints are as varied in flavour as the family is large, ranging from woody, musty sage to menthol-rich peppermint.

Some mint plants are known as dead nettles, which adds to an already confusing situation, being mints that look slightly nettle-like. Dead nettles, however, have characteristically mint-like square stems and, because they are not nettles, stingless leaves. Red dead nettle is one of the most common of these plants, and one of the most likely to be spotted in both urban and rural locations, and is probably growing in your garden or local park right now. The annual plants grow across lawns and disturbed land, covering areas with purple flowers right through even mild winters, when little else is in bloom.

The edible stems, leaves and flowers provide a boost of vitamin C, fibre and iron, and like many wild edible plants are also used in traditional herbal medicines for a range of ailments, including reducing chills. It isn't only people that benefit from the chill-reducing properties of the plant: bursting into bloom in mild winters just as hungry bees venture out from their hives and holes, the orchid-like flowers of dead nettle open to offer pollinators a drop of nectar to sustain them and keep them warm, as unlike the bees that feed from it, there is no sting in the tail of dead nettle.

Purple-pink, orchid-like flowers grow
amongst leaves, wrapping around the top
of the stem. Dead nettle flowers have a top
petal that looks like a hood, hanging over a
lower petal that splits into two; the flowers
provide important early food for bees and
are delicious in salads.

Triangular, hairy leaves grow
pointing downwards, hiding
the stem beneath top leaves
that turn purple as they
age. Young leaves can be
used in salads, older ones
as cooking herbs.

Short, square flowering stems grow in often
large clusters, up to 30cm tall. Young tender
stems can be wilted, and taste of sage and kale.

RED DEAD NETTLE

Dead nettles are easy-to-gather, nutritious additions to food through the year. The plants sit closely in flavour to sage, robustly musty and mineral-flavoured, and are best paired with other strongly flavoured herbs, such as sage, marjoram, mint or rosemary, or with sweeter flavours, such as figs, grapes, pears and apples. The young leaves and flowers can be added to salads and are best chopped finely into dressings. Stems are delicious sweated in oil or butter, or added to stir-fries, especially with ginger. The older leaves can be blended in pestos, soups and gratins with other iron-rich greens, including kale, purple sprouting broccoli and stinging nettles. Fresh or dried leaves, stems and flowers can be used to make kidney-supporting, chill-reducing tea.

GREEN BEAN SALAD
Serves 4 as a side dish

- ½ garlic clove
- 2 shallots, peeled
- 1 tbsp capers
- A handful (or 25g) young dead nettle plants
- 3 tsp Dijon mustard
- 3 tbsp olive oil
- 2 tbsp white wine vinegar
- 200g French beans
- Salt and freshly ground black pepper

Dead nettles make a fantastic ingredient in mustard vinaigrettes and are delicious served with any kind of bean salad, including French beans that, like dead nettle, reappear in late summer. This salad can be served warm or chilled.

1. Mince the garlic and finely chop the shallots, capers and dead nettle leaves and stems (reserving the flowers). Place all the chopped ingredients in a jar, cover with the mustard, oil and vinegar, seal and shake to emulsify, adding salt and pepper to season.

2. Place the beans in a pan of boiling water and cook for 4–5 minutes, until tender. Drain, then place in a serving bowl and stir through the dressing, finishing with a scattering of the flowers.

DEAD NETTLE AND GRAPE SAUCE

Serves 4

- 50g red grapes
- ½ apple, peeled, cored and chopped into small pieces
- 30g dead nettle leaves and shoots
- 50ml extra virgin olive oil
- Salt and freshly ground black pepper

Dead nettle and grapes combine to make a beautifully simple fruity dressing for roast chicken, beetroot or fig salads. Both figs and dead nettles share an aromatic compound called germacrene, which gives the plants their earthy flavours and pairs incredibly well with grapes.

1. Purée all the ingredients to a smooth pulp in a food processor; season with salt and pepper. Serve at room temperature.

DEAD NETTLE AND WILD GARLIC BUTTER

Makes 10 × 25g portions

- 50g wild garlic leaves
- 50g dead nettle leaves
- 250g butter, softened
- Zest of 1 organic lemon
- Salt and freshly ground black pepper

Wild garlic and dead nettle are amongst the earliest wild greens of the year. This butter can be frozen for later in the year, when wild garlic has disappeared, and is delicious melted onto mushrooms or steaks.

1. Finely chop the leaves and add to a food processor with the butter, lemon zest, salt and pepper. Blend until the butter and herbs are completely mixed together. Place the mixture on a piece of greaseproof paper and roll into a fat sausage-shaped parcel. Keep for up to a week in the fridge, or slice and freeze in portions.

WAYS TO USE WHAT YOU FORAGE

PLANTS TO USE IN RAW SAUCES, PESTOS AND SALSAS

Chickweed leaves, stems and flowers
Dock stems
Garlic mustard leaves, flowers and seed pods
Ground elder leaves and flower buds
Hairy bittercress leaves and tender seed pods
Hawthorn leaves
Hazelnuts
Horseradish roots and leaves
Nettle leaves
Oxeye daisy leaves and stems
Plantain leaves and flower stems
Red dead nettle leaves, stems and flowers
Sorrel leaves and stems
Tender spruce tips
Thistle stems
Three-cornered leek leaves and flowering stems
Wild garlic leaves and flowering stems

PLANTS THAT CAN BE USED IN SALADS

Bittercress
Chickweed
Dandelion leaves and flowers
Evening primrose leaves
Garlic mustard flowers and leaves
Hop shoots
Oxeye daisy leaves and flowers
Pineapple weed leaves and flowers
Red clover leaves and flowers
Sorrel leaves and tender stems
Tender mallow leaves
Tender spruce tips
Thistle stems
Three-cornered leek leaves, flowers and seeds
Wild garlic leaves, flower stems and flowers
Wild strawberry leaves
Young beech leaves
Young cleaver stems and leaves
Young ground elder leaves
Young hawthorn leaves
Young linden leaves
Young plantain leaves
Young yarrow leaves

PLANTS TO COOK AS VEGETABLES

Burdock stems
Common hogweed shoots and flower buds
Dandelion leaves
Dock leaves
Evening primrose leaves
Fat hen leaves and stems
Garlic mustard flower bud stems
Ground elder leaves and flower buds
Hairy bittercress
Hop shoots
Japanese knotweed shoots
Mallow leaves
Nettle tips
Plantain leaves and young flowering stems
Red clover leaves
Sorrel leaves
Three-cornered leek leaves and flowering stems
Wild garlic leaves and flowering stems
Young cleavers
Young horseradish leaves

PLANTS WITH EDIBLE ROOTS

Burdock
Common hogweed
Dandelion
Evening primrose
Garlic mustard
Hairy bittercress
Herb bennet
Horseradish
Mallow
Rosebay willowherb
Thistle
Three-cornered leek

PLANTS WITH SWEET EDIBLE FLOWERS

Blackthorn/sloe
Crab apple
Damson
Dandelion
Elder
Evening primrose
Gorse
Hawthorn
Honeysuckle
Linden
Mallow
Meadowsweet
Oxeye daisy
Pineapple weed
Rose
Rosebay willowherb
Thistle
Wild cherry
Wild strawberry

PLANTS WITH SAVOURY EDIBLE FLOWERS

Chickweed
Dock
Fat hen
Garlic mustard
Ground elder
Hairy bittercress
Himalayan balsam
Horseradish
Oxeye daisy
Red clover
Red dead nettle
Sorrel
Three-cornered leek
Wild garlic
Yarrow

PLANTS TO USE IN CONDIMENT SAUCES

Blackberries
Damsons
Elderberries
Garlic mustard
Hawthorn berries
Horseradish
Rose hips
Sea buckthorn
Wild blueberries

PLANTS TO FLAVOUR SALTS

Elderflower
Garlic mustard
Ground elder
Himalayan balsam seeds
Hogweed seed
Honeysuckle
Nettle
Oxeye daisy leaves and stems

Pineapple weed
Plantain
Red dead nettle
Rose petal
Spruce
Three-cornered leek
Wild cherry blossom
Wild garlic
Yarrow

PLANTS TO MAKE JAMS AND JELLIES

Brambles
Crab apples
Damsons
Dandelion flowers
Elderberries
Evening primrose flowers
Honeysuckle
Linden flowers
Meadowsweet
Rose hips and petals
Rosebay willowherb flowers
Sea buckthorn
Sloes
Spruce
Wild blueberries
Wild cherries
Wild strawberries

PLANTS TO FLAVOUR SUGARS

Honeysuckle
Meadowsweet
Rose
Spruce
Wild cherry blossom

PLANTS TO PICKLE

Blackberries
Burdock stems
Crab apples
Damsons
Dandelion flower buds
Elderflower buds
Evening primrose seed pods
Garlic mustard seed pods
Hop shoots
Horseradish leaf stems
Mallow seed pods (fruit)
Oxeye daisy flower buds
Rose petals
Rosebay willowherb shoots
Sloes

Spruce tips
Thistle stems
Three-cornered leek seeds
Wild cherries
Wild garlic flower buds and seeds

PLANTS TO FLAVOUR CORDIALS AND SYRUPS

Blackthorn flowers and sloes
Bramble buds and berries
Burdock roots
Crab apples
Damson blossom and fruit
Dandelion flowers and roots
Elderflowers and berries
Evening primrose flowers
Gorse flowers
Hawthorn blossom and fruit
Herb bennet roots
Honeysuckle flowers
Japanese knotweed stems
Linden flowers
Meadowsweet flowers
Nettle leaves and young stems
Pineapple weed flowers and leaf stems
Red clover flowers
Rose petals and hips
Rosebay willowherb flowers
Sea buckthorn berries
Spruce tips
Wild blueberries
Wild cherry blossom and fruit
Wild strawberries
Yarrow leaves and flowers
Young beech leaves
Young oak leaves

PLANTS TO FLAVOUR LIQUEURS

Acorns and oak leaves
Beech leaves and masts (nuts)
Birch twigs
Brambles
Burdock leaves
Cherry blossom and fruit
Chestnuts
Crab apples
Damsons
Dandelion flowers and roots
Elderflowers and berries
Evening primrose flowers
Gorse flowers
Ground elder
Hawthorn flowers and berries

Hazelnuts
Herb bennet
Himalayan balsam flowers
Honeysuckle
Hops
Horseradish
Linden flowers
Meadowsweet
Pineapple weed
Red clover
Rose
Rosebay willowherb flowers
Sea buckthorn
Sloes
Sorrel
Spruce
Thistle flowers
Wild blueberries
Wild strawberries
Yarrow

PLANTS TO USE IN BAKING

Acorns
Beech masts
Chestnuts
Common hogweed seeds
Dandelion flowers
Elderflowers
Evening primrose seeds
Gorse flowers
Hazelnuts
Herb bennet roots
Honeysuckle
Hops
Meadowsweet
Nettles
Pineapple weed
Red clover
Rose petals
Spruce tips
Thistle flowers
Wild strawberries
Yarrow

INDEX

AUTHOR ACKNOWLEDGEMENTS

I suspect I gave my parents quite a few worried moments during my childhood: I was the kind of child who fell out of a tree because I wasn't concentrating, or would be an hour late home from school because I was diverted by a road full of trees festooned in cherry blossoms. My school reports were littered with references to daydreaming and absent-mindedness. But my parents had a hunch I was actually wondering about things in my daydreams, and they encouraged me to keep it up. And I'm glad they did because I ended up by wondering all my life, mainly about the world around me and the rumbling of my tummy, which led by a series of very fortunate events to writing this book. Thank you to my Mum and Dad for allowing me to see the wonder in it all. (And sorry for all the heart-stopping moments wondering if I'd ever get home.)

When I left college I spent a few years struggling into striped suits, but I was never made for an office and in my mid 20s I began working in a day centre with older people, many of whom had grown up on farms, in some cases building their own. These inspirational people were gatekeepers to a new world of wonder – the world of wild food. From hours sat chatting with Patience, Mona, Dot and many more, I realized wild food wasn't just something that belonged in other countries, in the past or for a few romantic types – it was here, part of their food lexicon, just getting forgotten. Wherever they are now, I hope they're eating wildly well and I thank them for their unwitting contribution to turning me into an evangelist of eating weeds.

Forage definitely wouldn't have been published if the mind-reading Zara Larcombe at Laurence King hadn't approached me to write it, not knowing that I had been sitting on a proposal for 8 years, not daring to dial the number of a publisher in case my phone should combust as a result of the rejection. She worked tirelessly to turn our individual ideas of what a foraging book should be like into something I am very proud to have written; thank you for choosing me to do it. I have no other experience of a publisher to compare my editor Chelsea Edwards to, but if she is the norm, then the world of publishing is a lovely one; thank you for the encouragement, for your endless patience and for being the kind of person who it is a delight to see is phoning. Huge thanks to Maggie, Helena and Vanessa who have worked behind the scenes correcting, refining and laying out the book to make it read and look far better than I could have ever imagined. Thank you for all you have done; you are admired from afar.

This book wouldn't be half of what it is, quite literally, without the incredible illustrations from Rachel Pedder-Smith. Every time a file would arrive my whole family would crowd around the computer to see her new images – I am absolutely thrilled you were asked to illustrate the book. Whilst I wrote this book, a hero of mine, and someone I am very glad to call a friend, Mark Diacono, was often at the end of the phone, providing hours of advice and encouragement. Mark is not only a brilliant writer, gardener and cook, but he can now add mentor and counsellor to his CV – I'm very lucky to have your number.

My three girls were a couple of shoe sizes smaller when I started writing *Forage*. I've had to hide away for weeks, hearing them playing and sometimes arguing in the background. When my eyes ached from staring at a screen, they kept me writing, cheering me on. Thank you girls for letting me write this book, for your patience and for the day you told me you were proud of me for doing it – if you become mums one day, you'll know that the endorsement of your children is the biggest award you could ever win and I'm so proud of all of you and who you are becoming; thank you for being my wonderful, funny and kind girls. I love you more than every atom in every star in the sky (now tidy your rooms).

My husband is the kind of person it's good to be married to when you're writing a book. He's unflappable and calm and the most grounded of people I know – thank you for doing what you've always been marvellous at and getting on with everything whilst I have had to hide away typing. I love you Mr Knight.

Finally, thank you to everyone who has tasted my recipes over the years – my unsuspecting friends who've had spoons shoved into their mouths, guests who've eaten and cheered as courses arrive at wild feasts, those of you who've shared your own wild recipes and stories at markets, on foraging courses and online. The world is not just rich in wild food, but rich in people who generously share their knowledge – thank you to those people whose tale has woven its way into this book; you have made it more vibrant and more delicious.

LIZ KNIGHT is a British-based forager and wild food cook. She is the founder of the acclaimed Forage Fine Foods, a unique little food business that preserves the flavour of her local area, turning her finds into food for sell-out wild feasts as well as preserves that have graced the shelves of stores such as Fortnum & Mason. Alongside gathering and producing wild food, Liz has been teaching foraging courses for over ten years. She is passionate about teaching people that what might be seen as a weedy garden is probably, in fact, full of nutrition-packed, sustainable and utterly delicious food.